The Quarterly

Issue No.1
The Tomkins Times

Paul Tomkins, Chris Rowland, Andrew Beasley,
Daniel Rhodes and more

© 2020 The Tomkins Times

Table of Contents:

Introduction

The first quarter of the 2020/21 season was about as dramatic and incident-packed as any in living memory, especially when played against the backdrop of a global pandemic, with the campaign condensed into a much shorter period of time. Injuries, goals, penalties, controversies and shock results piled high across the division, as Liverpool sought to defend their title against the odds in the face of losing key players to severe injuries, inexplicable VAR interference and a schedule that pitted them against several key rivals and in-form teams.

This is the story – and analysis – of the first quarter, as told by the august (and in some cases, bald) writers of *The Tomkins Times*. This inaugural issue of *The Quarterly* gathers together a batch of the best pieces written as the season unfolded (a couple of which have been edited down), as well as several new chapters written specifically for inclusion in this book. As ever with our work, it is a mixture of match-going experiences, Liverpool history, empirical evidence and modern statistical analysis.

The book appears in the written chronological order, with the exception of an article about a surreal incident in 2011, which was penned in September 2020 but appears as the penultimate chapter.

Warning: may contain Jordan Pickford. Safety precautions are advised.

A New Rivalry For Our Times

By Chris Rowland

August 3rd 2020

It's been said that one thing Liverpool's fans and Manchester United's had in common is we both sang about Liverpool all the time! Well the same could now be said of Manchester City, as their obsession with the Reds has reached the point where it threatens to surpass even that of their neighbours (even one of their main songs is to the tune of a certain Liverpool band's 'Hey Jude'!).

Rivalries between fans of football clubs is hardly a new phenomenon, of course. Liverpool and Everton have been rivals forever. Well since 1892 anyway. To Reds residing within the Merseyside area, it's the only rivalry. They might see the Manchester lot four times a season when they play them, but they see Evertonians every day, in their workplaces, on their buses and trains, in their pubs and cafés, on the radio, the paper. It never goes away.

The further away the geography spreads from Merseyside, however, the likelier it is that Manchester United would probably take over as top rival. They're the ones with support everywhere, beloved by the media (as well as by referees and VAR this past season), a long period of sustained success just as Liverpool's came to an end – success, wealth, glamour, attitude, cockiness – what's not to dislike?

In the past, several other clubs have risen to become rivals-in-chief to Liverpool – Leeds United, Nottingham Forest and Arsenal have all also had their moments, though on a different level to Everton and Utd. Chelsea surged to the forefront more recently, the Jose Mourinho/Roman Abramovich era heralding a coarse loadsamoney culture that was and still is as far removed from Liverpool's DNA as any other club in the land.

And then came City.

But a City unlike any we'd ever known before.

City have never been serious rivals of Liverpool before. They had never really been important enough. They'd even been down to the third tier. As their neighbours became all-consuming, a money-making trophy-winning bloated behemoth, City were almost defined by not being them. Remember the book 'Man Utd ruined my life'? Written by a City fan. In the days when City's only rivals were that shower across town.

The City of then were the product of their Maine Road environment, down-to-earth, unglamorous, unsuccessful but sort of real, at least compared to their showbiz neighbours, hemmed in by the Coronation Street terraced rows of Rusholme and the flat-roofed graffiti-strewn badlands of Moss Side. I remember me and a mate going to a League Cup semi-final 1st leg there in 1981. Tucked ourselves into a pub called the Beehive, right opposite the Kippax where their 'boys' went. The Beehive had a fair percentage of them in it. We stood in the corner drinking Hydes Bitter and not saying much. Then someone burst in and shouted 'Specials are in!" The place almost emptied. Liverpool's football special trains – remember those days? – had arrived at Piccadilly, and they were all off for the fight. Scousers and Mancs. This was all part of matchday ritual back then. And City was by no means the most dangerous place to go. You'd have been more apprehensive going to Leeds, Birmingham City, West Ham, Chelsea, Utd or Spurs. We just stayed where we were, drinking.

City's fans then were known for their lugubrious, self-deprecatory black humour, borne out of a seemingly endless succession of failure and ridicule and false hope, of being locally second best and nationally irrelevant. If success didn't really suit them, it was perhaps just as well. Apart from a brief flurry in the late 60s/early 70s, Francis Lee, Colin Bell, Mike Summerbee et al, when they won a title, an FA Cup and a European Cup Winners' Cup, in the old adage they were modest and had a lot to be modest about. I remember after we'd beaten them 4-0 and 6-0 in the space of four days at Anfield in the League Cup and League in 1995, their fans inside the ground singing 'Alan Ball's a football genius' about their manager.

There's not much self-deprecation about any more.

First they moved out of Maine Road, and acquired themselves a new stadium for free, the Commonwealth Games stadium in East Manchester. A sheikh bought in, and the cash gushed in. City struck gold – or rather oil. Player after marquee player started arriving. They started competing at the top end, and winning things. Eventually, as the cash just kept coming, so did the trophies. The Premier League trophy in 2012, the first of four in eight seasons. After no title for 44 years, suddenly there was a glut, as well as any number of domestic cups of varying degrees of insignificance. Hell they were even counting Community Shields to help with the statistics to prove how great they were and how scared people were of them.

Just as significantly, a new breed of fans and a new attitude took root, drowning out the old school in a log flume of entitlement and expectation that came cascading down from the newly titled Etihad Stadium. The role of the media and pundits was to lavish praise on them, and the role of every other club and their fans was to be subordinate and know their place.

Upstairs, downstairs. They got used to having the run of the place, a strutting cockerel, going where and doing what it pleased.

Their 2017/18 title win saw them hit the 100 point mark for the first time in history. 32 wins, 106 goals, a 19 point gap to 2nd placed Manchester United, with Liverpool a distant 4th, 25 points behind. All that power complex and sense of entitlement just cranked up a notch.

You might think they would see Liverpool as nothing to worry about.

But something happened that season to change our relationship with City, possibly forever.

In April 2018, the teams were drawn against each other in the quarter-finals of the Champions League. The first leg, at Anfield, saw Liverpool eviscerate City with a three goal salvo that seemed to scar City, team and fans alike, psychologically. It bit deep. Witnessing the seething mass of delirium that was Anfield only deepened the cut. But perhaps more than anything, the encapsulation of that horror night for City – and they were definitely not used to things going this catastrophically wrong anymore – was seeing their team bus being attacked on its way to Anfield, hit by missiles thrown at it, damage done, windows broken (make their journey hostile and intimidating by all means but don't throw stuff at them!). I would imagine that would be very unsettling for the players just before such a big match, experienced internationals though they all were. Creating a hostile corridor full of red pyro and chanting, flag waving masses is one thing, but the actual physical damage handed them the moral high ground, as well as another reason to demonise the evil Scouse empire. And to be fair, we would not have reacted well if the roles had been reversed.

Their fans tried bravado, it wasn't over yet, the better team would still prevail, etc etc. But deep down they knew their number was up. You don't come back from 3-0 defeats in the Champions League!

Their very early goal in the return leg in Manchester raised their hopes. Falsely. Once Mo had equalised leaving them needing five, it was done. A 2-1 away victory for Liverpool saw us on the way to Kiev. And Kiev was to become a vital link in the fast-emerging rancour between the fans and the rapid descent of their relationship – that song, and their version of it.

Just as *Allez Allez Allez* became our theme tune for that season's march to Kiev, their deeply unpleasant version started to emerge, at City games against just about anyone. Singing about Liverpool when you're not playing them? Not cool.

Just a reminder, against my better judgment, of their version:

> All the way to Kiev
> To end up in defeat
> Crying in the stands
> And battered in the streets
> Ramos injured Salah
> Victims of it all
> Sterling won the double
> And the Scousers won fuck all
> Allez, Allez, Allez,

In terms of its obnoxious quotient, it ticked so many boxes – Ramos injuring Salah, check. A player they signed from us and who we routinely boo won medals and we didn't, check. The suspicion still lurks, and the possibility still irks, that the line about being battered in the streets referred to Sean Cox, whose incident happened in the first leg of the semi-final against Roma.

Some Liverpool fans take it as that, but the City fans I asked deny that and just say our fans got battered in Kiev (which is A Good Thing, presumably). To which I ask where they got that information from, because I, unlike them, was there, along with 50,000-plus other Liverpool fans, and I never saw a single one or heard of one, or knew of anyone who knew anyone, who had been battered in the streets. The locals could not have been friendlier or more engaging and helpful, but hey, you know best, stick with your version.

I accept there is a glaring inconsistency in attributing City's animosity towards us to the Champions League humiliation – City's fans' disdain for the competition and contempt for its organisers (which I suspect will miraculously vanish in the hideous event that they actually end up winning the thing). They still routinely boo throughout the Champions League anthem before games and turn their backs, a protest at what they perceive as persecution by UEFA. The way they see it, the elite establishment of European football don't like these brash newcomers, these gatecrashers, getting into their party. In their minds, they are outsiders breaking in, challenging the established elite, ragged street urchins sneaking past the doormen and taking their rightful place amongst the periwigged, face-powdered, beauty spot–painted prancing buffoons. The fact that these urchins have more wealth than virtually all those inside seems to elude them.

Jürgen Klopp's Liverpool now began to threaten City's domestic hegemony as, in 2018/19, Liverpool and City became proper rivals on the pitch as well as off it as they battled for the title in one of the best, most close-run title races in history. It certainly set records: Liverpool losing just one league game all season, winning their last nine games straight off and finishing on a colossal 97 points, the club's highest in a history which included 18 title-winning seasons, yet still finishing runners-up as City won their last 14 to snatch it by a single point. Suddenly the two clubs existed in a separate league to everyone else.

I witnessed first-hand the complete change in hostility and animosity directed towards us in two Liverpool games at the Etihad, in September 2017 and January 2019, with that Champions League tie, the one that I believe triggered the seismic shift between the two sets of fans and the teams themselves, in between.

The first was the one in which Sadio Mané was sent off and we lost 5-0. It was their 100-points title-winning record-setting season.

The atmosphere between the two sets of supporters, other than over the sending off incident when their keeper was carried off injured, wasn't noticeably different to previous times. But by January 2019, the degree of toxicity was off the chart.

On the pitch, we lost 1-2, and it was the game where the title was eventually settled. It was the game of Vincent Kompany (normally a decent, thoughtful and articulate human) towering over Mo, having just scythed him down and, instead of lying low and thanking his lucky stars he didn't get the red card he deserved, yelling 'pussy' at the prostate Egyptian king. It was not typical of the man, but like the rest and like the crowd, he seemed pumped up and ready for a fight. It was also the match where the ball only had to travel another 11mm for Liverpool to have scored another goal and possibly secured the title.

I wrote about it in a *My Day at the Match* for TTT at the time:

"The entire occasion seems orchestrated, not organic. But there's a wall of antipathy coming from beyond that segregation and throughout the ground. They sing the Gerrard slip song and

11

their twisted version of *Allez Allez Allez* with enthusiasm – wonder how the fans of a club that have never even been to a European Cup final feel they can deride one who's been to eight and won it five times? I'd feel a bit sheepish about it, but they don't seem in any way inhibited. There's a periodic surge from their fans towards ours, fended off by the Show Sec hordes, and both City's fans and some of ours are having eyeballing contests and 'you and me outside' kind of exchanges, constantly. It's not where I'd choose to sit, to be honest.

"The City team play like the crowd are behaving, fired up way beyond normal, and they feed off each other. The degree of sheer visceral hatred directed towards Liverpool, team and fans, is quite eye-opening. They are absolutely obsessed with us.

"The result was upsetting, but nowhere near as much as the wall-to-wall universal hatred and obsession their fans have towards us. It seems Everton, Utd, City, Chelsea and for some reason Spurs share this, but this was as intense as anything I've encountered at Old Trafford. We seem to do something that cranks them up several notches, and whatever it is, I sincerely hope it's NEVER GONNA STOP!"

What the Champions League tie, and the fact that we were seven points ahead of them going into that showdown at the Etihad, and that we pushed them right to the final day that season, and even had a hand on the trophy for a minute, confirmed was that City, an admittedly superb side even if they can't defend, now had a serious rival, a team that could match them stride for stride, blow for blow. A trend which reached delicious fruition last season when Liverpool left Manchester City and 30 years of hurt 18 points behind.

There were signs that Liverpool seemed to be getting to the City players as well as their fans, and the players' behaviour seemed of an abrasive bent that matched their fans. Footage emerged of City's players singing their bastardisation of *Allez Allez Allez* after they had finally seen off our challenge with the last day win at Brighton in May 2019, they first denied it and then apologised for it. There was more evidence of City's players' antipathy towards Liverpool over a year later when, as fate would have it, they became the next opponents for Liverpool after the Reds sealed the 2020 title. The peremptory, half-hearted guard of honour they offered was pathetic. It began to disperse before the whole Liverpool team had passed and Bernardo Silva, the snidey and overwrought Portuguese, couldn't even manage to offer a clap (and just imagine how indignant they'd be if the roles had been reversed! Typical disrespectful Scousers! Not big enough men to take it on the chin!). Liverpool had six more matches afterwards, and their opponents all offered proper guards of honour, even Chelsea, but City couldn't manage it. It's just a question of respect for your fellow pros, and they clearly don't have any.

It was not always thus. There was a time when there was no special animosity between the clubs beyond a base level Scouser/ Manc rivalry, which is about more than football anyway but about history, two cities' tussle for regional influence and dominance, the docks, the Manchester Ship Canal, the cotton and wool trades and all that.

That said, the antipathy between the two cities always seemed to me to be more westbound than east. In Liverpool, mentioning Manchester is likely to be seen as an admission that they're occupying your headspace, which you shouldn't. Generally. There is a huge cultural divide, in this respect among many others. In Manchester you're displaying your Mancness by slagging Liverpool at every turn. In Liverpool you're displaying your Scouseness by not mentioning the Mancs at all.

The two Gallagher brothers, of Liverpool tribute band fame and publicly paraded dumbness, entered the fray. Before the 2019/20 season began, a video appeared of Noel Gallagher holding up four of his six fingers to claim that's how many trophies City would win this season. Good shout Noel, the Premier League title (with City's blue and white ribbons no longer attached to it), the Champions League and the FA Cup have gone, but well done on winning the League Cup. Great prediction Noel. Gallagher went on to mock Liverpool for finishing with their record highest points total and still not winning the league, which was, he gloated, 'too funny'.

Finishing 18 points ahead of City, that was too funny as well.

Never one to be outdumbed, his brother weighed in by tweeting '#lfcchumpions after City beat the new champions at the Etihad. If a team that had already won the title and ended up finishing 18 points ahead of City could be called chumpions, it begs the question what does that make City? There are times to shut up and avoid increasing the size of target that you represent.

The two managers of these two clubs are unquestionably the best two in the Premier League, and quite possibly in club football worldwide. There is a rivalry there too, as they go about their business in such wildly opposing ways. Guardiola, intense, obsessive, sparky, doing his wild-eyed King-Lear-on-the heath impression, constructing his teams to play a style of football that is distinctive and aesthetically pleasing, in a one-dimensional sort of way. It sort of relies on having an inexhaustible supply of the best players, which the dubious bank-rolling by the oil-rich seems to assure.

Then Klopp: charismatic, smiley and huggy, but with a clear focus on what is needed and meticulous attention to detail across a whole range of areas and amidst a whole toolset of managerial attributes. Klopp's identity is intensity, as our own Pep (Lijnders) said – and his teams play a more rounded game than City's, they have more of a plan B, more different ways to win. A Klopp interview and a Guardiola interview are very different things to behold. You can imagine hacks looking forward to a bit of Klopp humour as a tonic, but taking a deep breath before a heavy session with Pep.

They may go about their business very differently, but they share common traits – a desire to create lasting success, almost obsessive drive in pursuit of their goals on the training pitch, albeit again very differently, a rehearsed and suffocating pressing game. Pep looking to establish the patterns, movement and passing till it becomes second nature, Klopp looking to weld together a group of strong characters who will work ceaselessly and stand shoulder to shoulder with each other on the pitch. Go easy in training at Liverpool and you're toast. Klopp is also willing to trust in a whole team of specialists in everything from transfers and player fitness to diets, opposition analysis and match day preparation, whilst Guardiola seems to need to be the lone conductor, directing the orchestra.

It seems likely that Pep will depart the scene before Klopp does, but at least one more season's head-to head would seem to await. Despite the claims of Chelsea, Man Utd and Arsenal, there has been a chasm between these two sides and the rest for the last few years, and it's hard to see it being closed in one bound. The two sides, the two managers and the two sets of fans look likely to be locking horns for some time to come as they compete for success on the pitch. On the pitch, the new rivalry is unlikely to fall away anytime soon. Off it, City may not be our greatest rivals but we're certainly theirs!

The Rise of Brilliance – What to Expect From the Premier League Title Race

By Mark Cohen

(Mark Cohen's annual preseason appraisal, published August 31st 2020)

In Christopher Nolan's 2008 masterpiece *The Dark Knight*, it is the manic Joker who explains the environment to The Batman.

He says, under great duress from the caped crusader, "There's no going back. You've changed things … Forever."

On 24 February 2020, Liverpool beat West Ham 3-2 at Anfield. A full 365 days earlier, Liverpool had drawn 0-0 at Old Trafford. Two fairly innocuous results but sandwiched in between had been a success rate unparalleled in top flight football.

In all, the record on the 24th February 2020 stood at 36 wins and two draws from the last 38 games. An astonishing return, and I believe – Liverpool had changed things – forever. In seasons past, it was accepted that a team could lose a game here and there, have a bad day at the office now and then, and live to tell the tale. In its early days, the winning team needed around 80 points, with the runner-up being close behind. Eighty points roughly equates to a 24-win season, with approximately half the other 14 games drawn. This allows for no less than seven defeats as an average. That's a lot of off days, that is.

Currently, a quarter of a century on from those numbers, a team needs more than 85 just to challenge. In the last three years, 95 wouldn't have been enough! The staggering win rates of the champions in this new period has seen 100 points hit, a 99, a 98 and a 97 in the last three seasons. Indeed, Liverpool have lost just four league games in the last two seasons. Extrapolating further, a paltry nine times in the last three seasons. That's nine losses in 114 games! Also, two of those losses came after having already been crowned champions. So really, just seven meaningful losses in 107 league games. Unparalleled.

Thing is, before Liverpool started racking these numbers up, it was Pep's Manchester City that were all about the records. A dozen years earlier, Jose Mourinho's Chelsea was the dominant force. The difference with those two, compared with Liverpool, is that they were achieved with a largesse which didn't so much beat as bewilder the rest. Mourinho's arrival brought with it the seminal phrase 'They're playing fantasy football – with live ammunition…' such was the crazy fees spent on rapidly building a squad.

City weren't much better, and their net transfer spend over the last five years according to *Transfermarkt* is over £600m (€669m).

The good news for Everton fans is that they've burned through a quarter of a billion Euros and have a squad that should easily challenge for top eight in 2020/21, but let's not digress too far from the article's subject.

The main takeaway for these purposes is that when the big guns rode into town, à la Chelsea in 2004 and City from when the Sheikh arrived (figuratively of course, he has only ever been to one match) in 2008, the rest had to essentially sit back and watch the fireworks for a season or two.

There was little the league could do in 2004/05, when Chelsea were breaking 100-year-old records on the way to their first crown in 50 years, and there was a similar resignation in 2017/18 when City barfed up 100 points. In Mourinho's first iteration, it was a rebuilt Manchester United who finally knocked them down, and indeed it is only they who could have done so. The league had become, at that point, a supreme grouping of two, followed by a collection of also-rans. From 2004 until 2011, the Premier League trophy had just two different ribbons on it, dark blue and devil red, and this hegemony was only stopped by City in 2012 following their ingloriously monied march up the table from 2008.

Thus we had arrived at a point in the Premier league evolution (superbly analysed by this website multiple times) in which it was fairly clear that a title-challenging team (Leicester aside) had to have a certain cost to it, and Liverpool were not likely to be at the spending level required.

By the end of 2017/18 City's exploits would have been seen as being pretty much identical to Chelsea's efforts thirteen years earlier, except it was worse as United didn't seem capable of a challenge the following season under Mourinho, who by that stage had become a pale imitation of his younger self.

This really left City starting 18/19 in a group of one.

Manchester United had begun to resemble an abandoned amusement park, possibly some type of Disney Jurassic Park, with mice and dinosaurs roaming the field in equal measure, whilst Abramovich had watched on in dismay as men with a wealth superior to his (and who didn't always appear to be abiding by UEFA's Financial Fair Play rules) had arrived with a bigger stick. Arsenal were well and truly mired, their stadium costs and failure to adequately replace Arsène Wenger laying bare a really crappy team and spirit, whilst 2015/16 lottery winners Leicester had regressed back to a decent non-title chasing level. Spurs had made a good fist of pretending to challenge for a title without ever coming close to anyone at the summit and Liverpool were entering the 29th year of a rebuilding programme.

For anyone watching the beginning of 2018/19, and imagining an outcome based on past analysis, there really could have been only one probability – City would again walk the Premier League, as there was nobody who could realistically mount a challenge.

Then Liverpool got 97 points. Liverpool also won the Champions League. City would edge the Reds in the league, yes, but in doing so would only create a burning hunger and desire for almost literal perfection in 2019/20.

No, the reason why the Joker spoke to Batman and not Superman was that it was Bruce Wayne who changed things. No super powers, no sugar daddies, no 5,000-1 dreams to reality. Liverpool changed things by being the smartest, not just in the room, but inside the entire building. It was this genius, flowing right through the club, from John Henry to Michael Edwards to Jürgen Klopp to the players to the fans, that created a team capable of winning virtually every league game, for a year.

It is almost as though, because of our myriad near misses over the years, Liverpool as a club accepted that nothing less than total and utter evisceration of the rest of the league would do. No dropped points, no settling for a draw, no respite. Win Win Win.

In 2019/20 Liverpool, under Klopp, became the finest club side in the history of English Football judged by being the fastest to the finish line – the most correct possible and sensible measure – and did it all legitimately, with a carefully constructed plan which took years to effect. Every single Reds fan should be proud.

Liverpool clinched the title with seven rounds to spare, and this mark was 40% better than the previous best of five, shared by Man City and Man United. Again, the context is vital – seven rounds represents 18% of the season, or nearly analogous to saying a sprinter crossed the 100m mark before any of the other runners had hit 85m … it's absurd.

Now, the reason why 2020/21 will be so different to previous versions is that it has dawned on the likes of United and Chelsea that they will need to be close to perfect to usurp both Manchester City and Liverpool, and this new truism creates a paradox – as everyone aims for perfection, the challenge of everyone winning everything becomes ever harder, and more points are dropped – even though the teams are aiming higher.

Gone are the days of waiting for a richly assembled Manchester United under Ferguson to put enough prolonged pressure on his adversary to see them off. Now it is, and will continue to be, the turn of Liverpool's analytics, rocket scientists and unsurpassed charisma which would have to do the trick, not to mention the mighty force of will which the entire red half of the city and fans around the globe pulled with as the title was sucked into the Kop with a record-breaking winning streak.

City were massacred in 2019/20, and to truly understand how torn asunder the entire league was by Liverpool, we need to appreciate that when City conquered all in 2017/18, they won the title by 19 points with little quality in their way.

Liverpool won the title by 18 points, in a league including a superb Manchester City themselves. To gain perspective on Liverpool's achievement, the 100m dash metaphor works again – it's similar to watching Usain Bolt smash the field by 15 metres in the 100m in a world record time, but then watching a chap named Red Bolt beat the Jamaican by 15 metres in the very next race!

Liverpool did this by attaining a level of perfection which is hard to fathom in league football. The three longest winning runs in English top flight history are 18, 18 and 17 games. What is remarkable, to the point of silliness, is that in 2019/20, Liverpool produced two of those back to back: 17 wins, a draw, and then another 18 wins.

In 2019/20 you could not drop a single point for months on end if you wanted to stay close to the Reds.

United, Chelsea and perhaps Arsenal, not to even mention City, know this only too well, and these three clubs are acutely aware that only long winning runs will do, if it is the title you seek.

Against this backdrop we enter 2020/21 – a year where the rise of brilliance will become apparent. It should be a titanic season with a much lower winning points total, as the quality of performance is shared out a bit more equally.

2020/21

In Premier League days of yore, we spoke of a big three – United, Arsenal and Liverpool. Some briefly rose up, Blackburn, Newcastle, Leeds and Leicester among them, but the first genuine addition was Chelsea, who were then joined by Manchester City and finally Spurs to create the fabled (and largely meaningless) 'Big Six'. It was essentially meaningless because, in almost every season, four of those members had bugger all designs on actually winning the title.

Things are different now, perhaps not in terms of having true designs on the title, as that realm surely remains closed to all but City and Liverpool next term, but in the overall dynamics of the table.

Firstly, I see 12 potential teams of quality. Not all with title aspirations, sure, but any of these could win five or six games on the bounce during the season and rocket up the table.

In a more egalitarian situation i.e. one where lots of teams can take points off each other, a run of six wins could be the difference in a successful season. It is worth remembering that City, the media 'champions' for their swashbuckling play and incredible talent oozing through their squad, lost nine league games including a 3-2 defeat at relegated Norwich in 2019/20. A quarter of their fixtures lost, so, rest assured, anybody can beat anybody.

Liverpool

Manchester City

Manchester United

Chelsea

Leicester City

Wolves

Arsenal

Tottenham

Everton

Newcastle*

Sheffield United

Southampton

These are the twelve teams of strong quality in the division with an asterisk placed by Newcastle pending their takeover. If it completes, which is now in grave doubt given the breakdown of the deal some weeks ago, then Newcastle will become, overnight, a threat. They won't challenge for top spots this year, but an influx of hungry younger and street-smart older quality players will likely mean plenty of wins against bigger teams this term, punctuated with the usual poor results as the team learns each others' traits.

It should also be noted that at the bottom of this list we have Sheffield United, a superbly drilled outfit, as well as the exceptional Ralph Hasenhüttl's Southampton – both of whom have exemplary qualities and methods and will too win their share of bigger games. That's 60% of the league who possess demonstrable quality.

Also think of the likes of Watford – a basement dweller who thumped Liverpool 3-0 back in February and were then relegated. Then remember Leeds United, a big club with an enormous history who will want to make their mark.

Anybody can beat anybody in a league of 'perfection'.

So it can be seen that, for the first time since we were all watching Hill Street Blues (we all were though, weren't we?), the league has a very even two-tiered feel to it. We've got a top ten or so, and a second ten. This will feel a lot more like a 1981/82 league table then a 2019/20 one, when all is said and done.

In that great bygone year, Liverpool would win the title with 87 points in a 42-game season (equivalent to just 79 points now), and the top 11 sides in the 22 team league would accrue 762 points. The bottom 11 – 503. This means the top 11 gained around 50% more points than the bottom group.

In 2018/19, the top 10 gained 689 against the bottom bunch's 380 – a difference of 80%! My big hunch is that the 2020/21 table in finality will closer resemble the old days' 50% than 2018/19's 80%, and it seems to be headed in that direction.

This makes a huge difference in the landscape and means that, for a title race to occur, consistency and an ability to produce results under pressure will be the difference between challenging and falling away.

There are four teams in 2020/21 with a better than 20% chance of winning the title: Liverpool, Manchester City;

Manchester United and Chelsea (% based on Bet365 odds 22-08-20). It's interesting that whilst bookmakers feel City remain favourites to recapture their crown (at odds of close to 50%), they also see United or Chelsea as about a 1 in 7 chance to stop them or Liverpool – a reflection of market forces and expectations more than statistical analysis.

Arsenal are also a little interesting, as under Mikel Arteta they should improve markedly and have a decent enough attacking squad, but probably won't come close to featuring in the title race. (By the way, the media loves a story, and Arsenal under Arteta has just such the comeback flavour they love. Their Community Shield win over the champions on penalties was greeted as a genuine sign of big progress, even though they were mostly battered in what amounted to a preseason friendly.)

Indeed, there was little mention of the gruelling nature of a Klopp preseason, designed as it were to create a base for the season to come, and not to peak in September. As Arsenal clung on bravely, Moyes-style, to a draw and subsequent shoot-out win, the media seemed to sense the narrative that Arteta was a man who Arsenal could build around. Whilst this may be true, and I think he has more promise than both Ole Gunnar Solskjær and Frank Lampard, too much is being read into Arsenal's defensive rearguard results against better teams with little to play for. They also didn't actually win the game, they drew, and some perspective is needed. Liverpool are calibrating, Arsenal are already firing everything they got, and once the league proper starts, this should become more obvious.

You can expect a lot of this fawning style coverage this term, every time somebody halts City and Liverpool's 'perfection'. Speaking of this domination, which the others will have to reign in, the numbers are stark; Manchester City remain a formidable unit, and will likely improve markedly over the summer through acquisitions. City's expected goal (xG) data is superb, and, on the face of it, remains well above Liverpool and the others'. Last season, City produced an expected non-penalty goal difference of close to double Liverpool's, and that even Chelsea's number was very close to the Reds'.

One of the major caveats, and probably the point at which xG reaches its limitations in this simple format, is that it ignores 'game-state', a vital component of analysis which paints Liverpool as a far more efficient team, with a similar probable goal difference to City and goes a long way to explaining where Klopp mastered the league in 2019/20. (Game-state is defined as: a team's xG at any given score, with the scores being split between being level, being one up or one down, or being more than one up or one down, so five states.)

Without going into too much detail, it's remarkable how good Liverpool are when the game is well and truly on the line i.e. when it's level, or one up or one down, as well as demonstrating how little time Liverpool spent behind in matches over the course of the season. Indeed, the only minutes Liverpool spent at more than a goal down last season were at Watford, with a 22 point lead at the top of the table at the time, and then at City, a match in which the celebrations of the previous week's title win were clearly visible in the lack of defensive focus for the performance.

Otherwise, it is clear that over the course of 38 games, City and Liverpool have the ability to dominate the important game states to be able to produce long winning runs which is why the two clubs have, by bookmakers' reckoning, an 85% likelihood of winning the title. Chelsea are also showing good numbers here, perhaps indicating they are closer to the top two than might be just assumed.

Importantly, it should also be noted by some work I did on a previous piece, that, when it counted, Liverpool's figures in the vital game states were far superior to City's. The analysis in the piece was done two thirds through the season, where Liverpool had amassed a virtually insurmountable 22 point lead over City. At that stage, Liverpool's goals for vs goals against when the game was in the balance was the game-changer. Liverpool had 27-4, City 23-10.

In other words – when the title race was nominally on, and both teams were under pressure to perform in order to win the thing, Liverpool absolutely thrashed teams – when the game was in the balance – whilst City didn't. Klopp's team had a +23 GD, City +13. That's nearly double, and shows clearly how much better the Reds were than them when it counted. Also remember City were the second best team in the country, and were being nearly doubled in this vital metric. They kept their overall xGD numbers strong by stuffing the odd team here and there, but what difference does it make if you win 2-0 or 5-0, if the following week you get beaten 3-2 at Norwich?

The other problem, and perhaps it will be City's achilles heel again in 2020/21, is that they tend to concede too many. Indeed, the Lyon quarter-final seemed to encapsulate their seasonal failings in 90 minutes – concede good chances, fail to protect the goalkeeper adequately, lose a game they should win. I'm not sure enough can change for them before next season begins, and as such, they remain vulnerable to bad luck and off days.

It all seems to suggest that Manchester City have padded their numbers well in the last third of the season where they had very little to play for and absolutely no pressure on them at all. This is borne out by the evidence that over their last 13 games where they scored 37 times and conceded just six (Liverpool had a

25-18 record, showing the foot was well and truly off the pedal by then). With the title no longer a possibility – how much did City's rampaging performances actually matter?

Beyond the consistency both sides are capable of, there are other key areas. First thought – how long will we have to endure matches behind closed doors or with vastly reduced capacities and atmospheres?

This is incredibly important beyond the mere awful aesthetic empty stands ensure. In my assessment of what might happen when football returned for the final nine rounds, I felt that two possibilities stood out:

– Better teams would whack lesser ones
– There would be fewer draws

Both of those proved accurate, albeit the draw difference is smaller than I expected.

Firstly, the top eight teams were winning over 60% of the games they played post-Covid vs a usual 50%, and this increase is a big difference, especially at the edges in a title race or relegation battle. If this environment remains it would greatly benefit a team like Manchester United who are without title-winning experience but are better than most of the teams they will play.

Secondly, draws were down by 12%, and this also creates a more binary outcome to a result – one or zero, win or loss. If a team is 'better' than its opponents, and the usual pressure of crowds don't apply, then the better team will win more often than not as they can simply get on with the business of being better without the additional stresses a crowd puts on their performance.

The conversion of draws to wins, and losses to draws can keep a team like United active in the title race for longer than they might have been, emboldening them and creating a virtuous cycle where success breeds success.

The exciting thing is that it looks like crowds will return fairly soon into the new campaign, as football is much the poorer without them, and if anybody thought their function was as mere spectators at a match before Covid, they can now see, with strong evidence, that fans are part of the fabric of a match, its outcome and its flow, and not just mutually exclusive viewers. Fans affect the outcome, but in ways that can be counter-intuitive.

Take United again. They've looked outstanding post-Covid, enjoying their football and finally offering a balanced sort of set-up, but how much of this will be impacted by an impatient Old Trafford, or a visit to a bustling Elland Road, now awaiting its first War of the Roses league encounter in a decade and a half? United have looked fluid and natural in this period, primarily because they can display their talents sans the stresses that a hugely expectant crowd will bring to bear. They have very good players, this is not in doubt, and they've got youngsters who are thriving on the training-like atmosphere that is prevalent.

Indeed, as the games ticked down and the inherent pressure of achieving 4th increased, so their performances became less natural, more stilted, more pressured. They also became fatigued, as Solskjær fielded similar starting XIs where possible but it's the pressure that is the big factor, even without crowds. Add them in, and you have a proper pressure-cooker mix of ingredients.

Mason Greenwood, a heck of a talent, scored 10 times last term, from an xG of just over 3.0. So he is scoring at a rate of three times better than expected. Either he is the love-child of Diego Maradona and Lionel Messi, with a sprinkling of Cristiano Ronaldo thrown in, or his numbers will regress markedly next term. I would think that much of his superb goal scoring efficacy is down to the palpable lack of stress that having no crowd offers. He can just get on with it, short back lift, hard follow through – goal.

The sooner crowds return next season, the sharper their effect will come into focus, and a team like United, with its youthful set up and recent upsurge, will feel this reversion acutely. At this stage it appears like an opening day fan return in reduced capacities is the target for the league, and, if safe, will be just wonderful to see come to pass.

But, and of course there's a but, Chelsea or United's title race, or Liverpool or City's, doesn't hinge on the twelfth man alone. A team will need more than a lack of atmosphere, or a crazy one, to win the title.

Now, let's get to the meat of it.

Title winning teams need consistency. City and Liverpool are streets ahead in this metric, and this is the one, above all else, that a champion makes. City have a consistency in being able to produce a glut of high quality chances – a certain bellwether for lots of wins, whilst Liverpool have almost perfected the art of winning the game itself. The two have differing styles, but for both, the goal will be long winning sequences and crucial results in their head-to-heads.

It is difficult to imagine Chelsea or United having the consistency to challenge, and it's basically as likely to imagine an Arsenal under Arteta finding great form and winning lots on the bounce as it is for Lampard and Solskjær's charges. There is not a great deal of difference between the three, except to say United and Chelsea have demonstrated a little more efficacy than Arteta's men slightly earlier.

It would appear that perhaps, one of them could challenge, by finding extraordinary form for a long period, and might even usurp one of Liverpool or City if circumstances were rare, but it's unlikely. United and Chelsea still appear to be trying to rely on an 'ends-domination' environment rather than an 'environmental-domination' one.

Ends-Domination vs Environmental-Domination

Ends-Domination: The attempt to control a game by controlling the one-on-one 'collisions' between players i.e. have strikers who take their chances better than your opponents, have goalkeepers who make saves when confronted in key situations, have defenders who make robust tackles on strikers and stop them at pivotal times. In other words – be better in the one-on-one situations that occur hundreds of times in a game on football (Mourinho a perfect example).

Environmental-Domination: The attempt to control a game by controlling the spaces the ball is allowed to be, by using the entire team (or environment) to create a pressure that is brought to bear on your opponents throughout the match (Klopp, of course).

The environmental system takes years to effect, to hone and to perfect. The ends one is quicker, as it relies on purchasing good players and letting them get on with it, which is often more than enough to beat the league's lesser lights regularly and shoot your way up the table.

Both systems can be good, and there is always a huge overlap between the two, but the environmental one is probably better for settled teams as it constructs them to play a lot of the game by rote, with the 'system' doing much of the work allowing the players' individuality to flourish as opposed to being reliant on their individual ability entirely.

The environmental system, when perfected, brings about consistency as one of its main off-shoots.

Consistency then, as United and Chelsea are trying to discover, is generally born of stability, and FSG has turned the club from being one of 'churn' to one of 'earn' over their ten year tenure. Under Klopp, Liverpool earn the right to results through a mix of superb tactical drilling, patience, fitness, an ability to understand the game state and react accordingly, and a very high skill set of the players, some of which Klopp inherited when he bought them and some of which the genius then coached into them.

Indeed, the point could also be made that Klopp has now either bought or coached players who would now end-dominate anyway – that is to say, Alisson is better in the key one on ones than the strikers he faces, and Mo Salah, Sadio Mané et al, are better than the keepers they have to beat to score. Van Dijk is almost always the victor in a one-on-one duel with a forward.

If true, then Liverpool are an environmental masterclass, who also have better players.

City, on the other hand, are not as good as Liverpool environmentally, although still strong, but also have ends-players who are generally better than their opponents. City have lots of them in the attacking half of the field but actually have very few defensively, new signings notwithstanding. Ask yourself honestly who of City's back five plus holding midfielder you'd consider for Liverpool and the answer is surely only a fully fit Aymeric Laporte.

And that's the thing – Liverpool have an extraordinarily good first 11, it's better balanced than City's, and perfected to its task of high but focused pressing.

Past are the times of Liverpool losing a key player or two every year, or at the very least of having a huge loss of focus as the player's head was turned. Instead, we now have a picture of serenity, a squad confident in its ability to deliver this ability every game. Indeed, the serenity is so marked that in 2020/21 it could turn out to be a problem, in that, because of Covid, we've been unable to add to a squad when it's at the top – a key deliverable in Alex Ferguson's recipe, and before that, Bob Paisley's.

Will we find ourselves a little too comfortable in our positions at the club next term? Will this lead to complacency? I'd like to think not, but it is a potential issue, and Klopp must make sure that he keeps the focus extreme to avoid that pitfall. It does seem as though the club, secretive though they are, intend on picking up one, maybe two players of high quality, with Thiago Alcântara mentioned plenty and the young Ismaïla Sarr from Watford seemingly on the radar.

These signings would beautifully augment a formidable unit, with the Alcantara one specifically a signing which will likely maintain the Reds' competitive advantage for the coming season given his extraordinary talent on the ball, in possession and out, alongside his knowledge of a pressing type of game which Bayern do nicely. Sarr would add good, young cover to the forward line. He looks a player with all the right attributes for Klopp – speed, balance, power, technical quality and a good attitude.

We don't need much, and we won't buy much.

City have the opposite position. Given they've now been given the all-clear to buy their way to every conceivable title they want from next year on, and the older age of their squad, it's fair to expect them to spend a bucket load of money. Pep's record in the transfer market is patchy, for every Ederson there are a handful of sub-standard full-backs, but I don't doubt the club's ability to procure talent in a market where they are one of the very few operating with both financial and legal impunity. If City can purchase players who immediately settle in, then they will be utterly formidable once more, the toothless carcass of FFP lying in their light blue wake, Raheem Sterling's tiny footprints the only thing between it and Manchester City as they hurtle towards 100 trophies.

Advantages

Liverpool hold a big advantage going into 2020/21 in terms of fitness and this can be summarised into four points:

A three month Covid break is probably the best thing that could ever happen for a hard-working Klopp team long term. The team will greatly benefit from the forced rest at the business end next season. I cannot think of a way in which this could be worse for the rest of the league – the fittest and best trained team got to have a collective 90-day break.

Klopp is the league's best coach in producing fit teams capable of playing 90 minutes of focused, honed football.

Liverpool have had nothing to play for post-Covid with the league secured early. Whilst this had led to the utterly predictable loss of form and focus, it has also had the upshot of having us play games with a preseason training ground intensity, which will help immeasurably later on next season.

By contrast, Chelsea and United have played every game with proper Premier League fixture intensity due to Champions League qualification concerns, whilst City under Pep have only one speed and it's real quick. City also had the Champions League tournament to play in August, another failure which will sap their energy for the next term with them only (already!)

returning to preseason training yesterday. It will give them an early boost perhaps, in terms of match readiness, but the long term effect will be brutal, even on a squad as huge as theirs.

Dynasty

Jürgen Klopp wants to create a lasting dynasty at Liverpool, and is clearly determined to do so. With competition this fierce though – all of City, Arsenal, Chelsea and United should improve markedly, and we haven't even mentioned strong squads like Tottenham or Wolves, it might be a tough season for the Reds on the silverware front. I'd be satisfied with a strong Champions League run, giving us dreams of Istanbul (just won't go away, hey), and a nice title defence taking us into the last few weeks of the season with number 20 still on the line.

If Liverpool can stay close to City, or United and Chelsea if they surprise, then I would think our longer pre-season rest, our fitter team and unbeatable mentality could be the difference again.

Klopp's team's absolute relentless brilliance over the last two seasons has raised the performance bar for everyone, and its effect on the league table will be big, pushing the likes of Chelsea and United to new personal bests whilst also galvanising behemoth Manchester City. They are all going to try and take us down. To stay top is the biggest challenge yet.

Under this wonderful manager, we absolutely could go on and win the big things again next term, but even if we don't, I am confident of a marvellous season and a thrilling ride.

It wasn't ever thus.

Von Mentalität Geführt.

Beyond Doubt – Liverpool Now Have Their Strongest Squad Ever

By Paul Tomkins

September 23rd

Going into the new season, it felt like Liverpool had a squad of peak-age senior players (plus the unmeltable James Milner, aged 57) and a clutch of emerging top-class youngsters. The addition of The Greek Lad™ (aka Kostas Tsimikas) solved the left-back cover issue whilst adding an option who can cut *infield*, while Curtis Jones usurped Adam Lallana. With Dejan Lovren also exiting, the club had options to cover at centre-back already in the squad.

This was basically the Champions League and title-winning squad, just now at peak age, instead of below peak age; with added cover to one position. It was experienced, but still full of hard-running, and it had the advantage of 2-3 years of team bonding and wavelength propagation.

Then, *last Friday happened*.

What a weekend it was for new recruits. The two new additions surely take the squad to the highest level ever seen at the club, and one looks likely to do the near-impossible, and improve the first team.

I actually had my first weekend away of the year (with my son and my dog, and some glorious weather), with my Leicestershire town having been locked down longer than any other, and due to go back into lockdown two days after we returned (ergo, now). We didn't go far, for various reasons, but as soon as we got to our destination in another part of Leicestershire I saw that Thiago was a *confirmed* signing. I hadn't packed my laptop, in order to avoid falling into the trap of working (and writing is always a temptation, as *football never sleeps*), but of course I ended up checking the news on my phone, and posting some comments on TTT with my thoughts via my clunky thumbs.

Within a few hours it seemed – via the throbbing grapevine – that a second major signing would be announced, possibly even later that night; and one that came out of nowhere. The good news was that having no laptop meant I could not be tempted into wasting some precious father-son bonding by writing 5,000 words on the brilliant potential of Thiago Alcântara and Diogo Jota. There was also even time for one of my favourite prospects, Ki-Jana Hoever, to head in the opposite direction to Jota.

As far back as February, I inadvertently stumbled upon the fact that Liverpool were "tracking" Jota (he ranked highly on Liverpool's scouting system), which I shared with one person on the TTT staff at the time and left it that. Obviously it's not my business to publicise any insider info I very occasionally find myself privy to (and I'm not someone who seeks this info, as I'm not a journalist hunting for stories, just a totally independent if obviously Liverpool-biased football writer/analyst), but I thought it would not be breaking any confidences right now to confirm on this site that this was not some random left-field signing, even if I naturally assumed back at the start of 2020 that the wealthily-backed Wolves project was not going to sell someone so good. While Jota wasn't at Sterling levels of "ungettable", he was a Portuguese player in a quasi-Portuguese club, who always seemed keener on buying than selling.

Indeed, it's increasingly tough to buy from the Big Six rivals, plus there's Everton, who are maybe the 7th or 8th biggest club (especially after new investment and with a big-name manager), who also never sell to Liverpool. Wolves seem like a club that was only going to ramp up its investment in the team.

And whilst my insider info may be sporadic (in the 11 years I've been running this site I've spoken privately to managers, owners and people in pretty much every other role at the club), I never use that to profit personally, and never sell subscriptions based on gossip. And as I note from time to time, I am only ever contacted first by people at the club, rather than me approaching them.

Indeed, this site doesn't do transfer gossip, beyond reporting the more credible rumours that are out there, and perhaps running the rule over them with some scouting software. We exist to try and analyse and explain (and crack the occasional crass joke). Sometimes someone at the club will find something interesting in what either I or others on the site are doing.

The reason there are so few leaks about Liverpool targets is because the club does not go around publicising the players on their radars. In this case, my info that Jota may have been a target certainly didn't get leaked; first, it would be a betrayal of trust, and second, it would perhaps jeopardise the move. We aim to be honest and level-headed, and we try to be intelligent and insightful … and *occasionally* we may even achieve that.

So it was nice that Jota was both an unexpected signing, but one that was clearly not some knee-jerk reaction by the club. His numbers stacked up well against those of Sadio Mané.

And at age 23, he is a quick and versatile goalscoring attacker, who can play anywhere across the front three, and, like Mané and Mo Salah at 23 (and Roberto Firmino, too) has scope to get better still under the guidance of Jürgen Klopp and co..

While the Jota move emerged out of nowhere, Liverpool's interest in Thiago Alcântara appeared back in the summer, but it also felt like it may be a reach; after all, he was at the club that were about to become joint German and European champions, who have a monopoly on the best players in the Bundesliga and no financial imperative to sell. But in the end, with one year left on his deal, sell they did. And £20m was an absolute bargain, even at the age of 29.

His debut was one of the best 45 minutes you'll see of passing and ball manipulation, albeit with an unlucky penalty concession thrown in. None of the three or four killer passes he tried quite came off, but it was only due to desperate defending, or the pass being a fraction overhit – almost like hitting the bar four times with amazing shots. All this after just two training sessions. While Jordan Henderson hit the pass of the game (not for the first time in recent seasons), Thiago is almost in a league of his own in that art.

It's also worth noting that he was hitting these attempted killer passes against a Chelsea team that had ten men behind the ball in the second half, in contrast to the one Henderson hit, where Mané had the whole of their half to run into. Alcântara joins the existing "quarterback" passers of Trent Alexander-Arnold, Virgil van Dijk and Henderson himself, with Fabinho another who can hit a glorious 40-yard ball, if perhaps not with the whip and fade and fizz of van Dijk and Alexander-Arnold (while Alisson is able to ping it long, and Andy Robertson has a useful flank-to-flank rangefinder).

Alcântara is now another, and while that may mean fewer longer passes by Liverpool's playmaking right-back, it could also put the young Scouser into more advanced crossing positions, as he finds himself in space as the opposition players have to start heading infield to get numbers around Thiago. The speed, range and disguise of the Brazilian-born Spaniard's passing in that 75-

touch second half at Stamford Bridge was a joy to behold, and while Henderson, Fabinho, Naby Keïta, Gini Wijnaldum, James Milner and others can all hit a lovely longer pass into the front three (or beyond them into the space, a la Henderson to Mané that led to the red card), Thiago just does so with even quicker thinking.

And while his playmaking skills are like those of Xabi Alonso, he has the terrier-like pressing and ball-winning of Javier Mascherano. If he can look after himself in the way that Milner and Man City's Fernandinho has, he could easily spend five years in the Reds team; indeed, as his body slows he'll still have that insanely good passing ability, and physically he doesn't look the type to suffer premature ageing – he's not heavy-set like a Wayne Rooney, nor has he played the number of games that someone like Rooney had as he melted in his late 20s. Contrast that to another United player, Ryan Giggs, who was lean and wiry. Rooney had played over 600 games by Thiago's age; Thiago has 396 club games and "just" 39 for Spain.

Thiago's talent was clear from a young age, but Barcelona and Spain had the best midfields in the world a decade ago (and as such, I assume he made quite a few substitute appearances earlier in his career), but even now he's never played more than 30 league games in a season, in part due to niggling injuries that hampered him at the time, but which now leave fewer miles on the clock. (Plus, seven years in Germany meant a maximum of just 34 league games per season anyway.) Equally, he's had five seasons of 40-50 games in all competitions, with many of those in the Champions League, so he's not incapable of staying fit.

But one bonus of this move is just what it does to Pep Guardiola's head. While I don't want to spend too much time this season worrying about what City or anyone else do, this is a player who was once Pep's crown jewel. He was the playmaker he pinpointed to take to Bayern Munich in 2013, and when Thiago got seriously injured in 2014, he turned to Alonso – which makes for yet another parallel between the two. Thiago returned to fitness in 2015/16 to return to the team alongside Alonso, and presumably Guardiola would have loved to take Thiago to City, for a third time working together, but Bayern were not a club that even Man City could raid (indeed, Bayern raided City this summer for Leroy Sané).

Equally, you wonder if Thiago was probably a bit worn down by the relentless but joyless Catalan manager. But what Guardiola and his team will see is an elite player – a world-class playmaker – who has just gone to the team they finished 18 points adrift of months earlier. Going back three years, Liverpool chased City; then hunted them down; then overtook them; then left them in their slipstream. And as good as City clearly remain, you wonder if this signing can have an adverse psychological impact on them, not least as they just lost their own talismanic Spaniard, David Silva, in addition to the mercurial Sané, having seen their on-pitch leader Vincent Kompany leave just over a year ago. And while Liverpool are not signing players to mess with City's heads, any demoralisation will be a bonus.

And if it seems like Liverpool now have too many midfielders, never overlook the versatility of at least half of them. Regular readers will know that I've long touted Fabinho as a potential centre-back great due to his skillset, but also, I felt that Joe Gomez looked like the future of Liverpool, alongside van Dijk. That hasn't changed. However, perhaps since the way Sterling was allowed by England to bully him, and his generally passive nature, Gomez found his confidence rocked at the Etihad when the Reds' ex-winger "used" him to win a penalty, as Liverpool eased off after winning the title. Sterling seems like a wily, manipulative character, whereas Gomez is just quiet and humble; but despite being the victim, it was Gomez who was booed by England fans. That can't be easy.

By the time the Reds lost at the Etihad, as highlighted by Andrew Beasley, the Reds' midfield wasn't really doing the hard-pressing of before (although that's back to normal this season), and so the defence was more exposed; van Dijk and Alisson also got a bit sloppy. But at just 23, Gomez – with just over 100 games for the Reds – is still a rookie for a centre-back. He has bounced back from previous dips in form to hit the heights that helped Liverpool win 27 of the first 28 league games of last season, and his partnership with van Dijk remains outstanding once you remove low-stakes games.

But Fabinho is an interesting alternative, not least as Thiago is a more creative holding midfielder. The two could obviously play in the same midfield, but it's another example of the incredible versatility that Liverpool look for. Theoretically, Fabinho could easily be a better centre-back than anyone in the top division bar van Dijk; his performance at Chelsea, as against Bayern Munich two seasons ago (another clean sheet, that time when deputising for the Dutchman), is part of an impressive, if small, sample size.

But anyone who is 6'3" and who began life as a full-back, and who moves to become a defensive midfielder, should be *ideal* for centre-back, unless exceptionally slow – and while no sprinter, Fabinho can cover the ground. Jamie Carragher, was only 6'0" and himself (before his legs gave out) swift rather than rapid, and had much the same trajectory; and at 26, Fabinho is at the exact ripe age I have always marked down for when centre-backs start to really look the part. He also has the added bonus of almost always being at match-speed; the way that he'll otherwise be starting games in midfield, and that's often easier than bringing in a totally cold centre-back who is 4th choice (as Joël Matip, Gomez and Lovren often found, when taking games to get up to speed). That's why Klopp has generally kept a smaller but more versatile squad, but this season presents new challenges.

The season is more compacted, meaning more games in less time. Rotation is going to be even more necessary, it would seem. The potential need to quarantine players is another reason bigger squads may be necessary; if you get a cluster of five players who all have to isolate for 14 days, that could encompass four league games, especially during the festive period. Add suspensions and perhaps the greater likelihood of injuries (with less rest time built into the season), and this could be a unique campaign. Even then, it doesn't feel like a *bloated* squad, but there are now several players who can be sold, released, loaned or sold-to-buy-back.

All of this leaves the Reds with the best squad the Reds have ever had (in part because the squads during earlier periods of success were much smaller); with a long list of emerging talent that will either be developed at the club or, whilst being closely monitored, elsewhere.

Quite how long the stars can keep aligning this perfectly – albeit in no small part due to the vision the club has implemented – remains to be seen. The transition between what will be six or seven ageing players in 2022/2023 to their replacements will likely be difficult, no matter how well planned; Klopp may not stay much beyond that point; the transfer magic may wear off simply through the law of averages and/or bad luck; and the recently kneecapped Financial Fair Play may be taken out at the waist, so that it has no legs at all.

But no club seems better set to thrive right now.

How Pressing Is The Key At Both End Of The Pitch For Liverpool

By Andrew Beasley

Note: this is a mixture of two articles, written several weeks apart.

Andy Robertson passed the ball to Sadio Mané, as he so often does. The Senegalese striker then played it past Reece James' right side and set off to his left. But Bobby Firmino wasn't sharp to the potential pass, and Fikayo Tomori got there first.

Whether he was annoyed with the number nine or himself, Mané was clearly frustrated. He didn't let it bother him though, and set off towards the Chelsea penalty area. At the point Tomori laid a simple pass back to his goalkeeper, Mané was two or three yards from the corner of the Blues' box. No matter the distance, he set off in a straight line to close Kepa Arrizabalaga down. You never know what might happen, right?

As he passed Firmino, the Brazilian pointed towards Jorginho, his countryman providing the most likely pass option for the Chelsea 'keeper. Mané changed the angle of his run, blocked Kepa's pass, and was able to slot the ball into the largely unguarded net. Press the opponent, recover the ball, and almost certainly wrap up the game; Jürgen Klopp heaven.

While this example from Liverpool's 2-0 win at Stamford Bridge is one of the best you'll ever see, it's hardly a first for the Reds. Indeed, I looked into their prowess for provoking errors in a TTT article almost three years ago. But data has moved on since then, so we're now able to look into how many mistakes the opposition makes per press, and what the expected goal value of the subsequent shots is.

Oh and, in case you didn't notice, Liverpool won the league last season, so it's probably worth looking into how crucial these opposition blunders were along the way.

Thanks to the *Statsbomb* data on the excellent FBRef.com, it's easily possible to see how many defensive errors – which are defined as: "when a player is judged to make an on-the-ball mistake that leads to a shot on goal" – a team both makes themselves and benefits from via their opponents. In the 2019/20 Premier League, Jürgen Klopp's side provoked the joint-most errors (21), along with Southampton, and had the joint-best error difference, tied with Manchester United (+11).

It seemed reasonable to assume that the more pressing a team did in the final third, the more errors their opponents would make. It cannot be entirely coincidental that Liverpool and the Saints were the top mistake provokers when they were also the top two teams for the number of pressures made in the opposition's defensive third.

There is also a reasonable degree of correlation between those statistics across the whole division. But where those figures have a Spearman's rho of 0.661 (where 1 is perfect positive correlation and 0 is random), the statistics for teams being pressed and making errors only has a rho of 0.221. However, that difference is to be expected. A team's own pressing and errors they provoke is the result of their hard work on the training ground, and the telepathic relationship which exists between their players. The pressing against them in an individual match is the result of that, but across a season it is a mishmash of what 19 different teams (and 22 managers in 2019/20) offered up.

It's also interesting that where *Statsbomb* recorded 21 opposition errors for Liverpool, Opta had 33. The former had 265 for the division as a whole, but the latter had 366, and this despite them having similar definitions. It's not that either is definitively correct, as it is, after all, a subjective statistic. One can only presume that *Statsbomb*'s definition is tighter; they had Sheffield United and Wolves both keeping error clean sheets when hosting the Reds last season, where the Premier League's official data partner had them making four and three respectively. Quite the difference.

However, as it's possible to get error times and locations from Opta, we'll be using their data for the rest of our study into attacking pressing, combined with *Statsbomb*'s shot involvement and shot distance numbers.

When dealing with the numbers, you could make a case that Liverpool either over- or under-achieved when it came to converting their opponents' defensive errors in 2019/20. The average conversion rate over the last nine seasons from chances such as these is 36.4% – almost identical to the rate for a clear-cut chance, as the two obviously overlap a lot of the time. On that basis, a team provoking 33 errors as Liverpool did could expect to generate 12 expected goals from the chances, and obviously net as many. The Reds fell considerably short of that total, as the shots were collectively worth only 5.8 xG. And they 'only' scored 10 goals, hence why they overachieved (in terms of xG conversion) but also underachieved (as they might have created better chances following the errors).

But perhaps this analysis is too harsh. The average value of a non-penalty shot taken by Liverpool last season was 0.12 expected goals, and for chances following errors it was 0.18. Thanks to the data on FBRef.com, we can also consider the distance from which the shots were taken from, and the ones from the same length from goal which were not gaffe-powered averaged 0.13 expected goals. The Reds were able to get better quality opportunities than normal from the locations they shot from when an error had led to the chance, and that always has to be the aim.

On the last occasion we looked into this aspect of the game, Mohamed Salah had been involved in the most shots following errors. And he was once again in 2019/20, but now that we can factor in expected goals, it was Mané who proved to be more important.

Liverpool had eight post-error chances worth 0.31 expected goals-or-more last season, and their Senegalese star participated directly in five of them, including goals against Burnley, Newcastle and Everton. His total xG involvement for error-related shots was 3.01, comfortably ahead of the tallies posted by Salah (2.28) and Firmino (1.28). We can add Mané's recent goal at Stamford Bridge to his ledger too, which – after only two matches, admittedly – is the highest value chance Liverpool have had so far this season, even including Salah's spot kicks against Leeds.

While Kepa's blunder only helped to seal the result at Chelsea, it's remarkable how many of the goals which followed defensive errors proved to be important to the outcome of matches last season. Aside from Mané's goal at Turf Moor, which was the second in a 3-0 win, the other nine were split as follows: four broke the 0-0 deadlock, three were equalisers, one put the Reds in front having earlier been behind (against the Magpies at Anfield) and one eventually proved to be the decisive goal in a 2-1 win at Southampton. The journey to the league title may not have been as relaxed over the second half of the season were it not for these 10 goals.

Liverpool scored four league goals in the opening six minutes of matches last season, and three of them followed defensive hiccups. They certainly showed the value of a fast start. And I assumed that opposition fatigue might play a part in them making mistakes, but it didn't particularly – only one of the eight high value chances even occurred in the second half, never mind late on in the game. But then a thought occurred: there are two halves of football, so two opportunities for fatigue. And sure enough, three of the big chances after errors occurred in the final 11 minutes of the first half. By the end of the match the result might be settled, plus Liverpool won't be pressing as ferociously due to their own exertions to that point (and how I wish we had pressing numbers by game state and time played).

But the result is likely still on the line at the end of the opening 45 minutes, and the Reds' fitness is probably still giving them an edge over their opponents at that point. In this compressed and compacted 2020/21 campaign, it will definitely be worth keeping an eye on this. Last season suggests such moments could prove vital to Liverpool's title challenge.

Nonetheless, this is a very well established facet of how the Reds attack and attempt to undermine their opponents. Liverpool might have made the most final third pressures of any Premier League team in the last three seasons in 2019/20, but they also topped the division's rankings for the two preceding campaigns too. It's at the back of the team where an evolution appears to be happening, and is therefore perhaps worthy of even greater scrutiny.

After all, if you're going to make an omelette, you're going to have to have some frank and honest discussion with the eggs. Liverpool have swept aside all comers from England and Europe at times in the last two or three years, but it wouldn't have been possible if they had been playing safety first 'Hodgeball'. To win 196 points over two seasons, you have to take a few risks.

And when you've got arguably the best goalkeeper and centre-back in the world, you can afford to. Except that the Reds are going to be without the latter for the foreseeable future, while the former seems annoyingly prone to semi-regular injuries.

But perhaps they needed to tweak the system slightly irrespective of those players' absences anyway. Virgil van Dijk played at Villa Park recently and it didn't stop Liverpool conceding seven goals there.

Seven? Seven. It still doesn't seem quite real, does it?

There have subsequently been countless articles on the Reds' high line and the problems which it can bring. A piece on *Sky Sports* ahead of the Merseyside derby highlighted that the back four aren't just a long way up the pitch this season, but even further up than they were in 2019/20. As the article also noted though, Liverpool's risky defensive system can certainly be effective when it works.

"The starting distance of their passing sequences – the most reliable measurement of where a team is positioned on the pitch – averages over 49 metres from their goal. Last season, Liverpool topped the league for this statistic, but with an average starting distance of 45 metres.

"The Reds' high line helped catch opponents offside a league-topping 142 times last season – no other team surpassed three digits and the league average was only 64."

And a heat map in the article for the 2020/21 season made clear that Liverpool's defence has been conducting the majority of its business near the halfway line, with two brightly glowing orbs either side of the centre circle lighting the way to Liverpool's average defensive position.

The *Statsbomb* data from last season (via FBRef.com) illustrates how this has far less potential to be a problem when

Becker is between the posts. Only three goalkeepers across Europe's big five leagues – one of whom was former Red, Péter Gulácsi – averaged more defensive actions *outside* of their penalty area per 90 minutes, and only two made interventions further from their goal on average. Manuel Neuer was the only stopper ahead of Alisson in both categories, and he's not a bad sweeper keeper to measure yourself against, is he?

Adrián is nowhere near as proactive. He averaged 0.72 defensive actions beyond the safety of the penalty box per 90 minutes in his first season with the Reds, with the average distance from goal of such actions being 13 yards. For Alisson, those figures were 1.31 and 17.3 respectively, illustrating why he is a 'top of the class' sweeper keeper whereas his Spanish deputy prefers a safety first approach. The return of the former Roma man in goal will clearly help to prevent certain problems which a high defensive line can bring. But it also seems too simplistic to blame the horror show at Villa Park upon the back four alone, as culpable as they obviously were.

Defending near the halfway line only really works if the players in front of the back line can prevent the opposition from making incisive passes through and beyond it. As an article from *Liverpool Offside* noted:

"Should the opposition find their way through the primary press, some control has been lost, and the balance begins to shift towards damage limitation, through the *secondary press*. Here, the full-backs and/or midfielders, depending on the location of the ball, will do their best to disturb the ball carrier, ideally forcing play to go backwards, but at the very least, making sure that a clean look at a through ball is avoided."

Sounds straightforward enough. But against Aston Villa, it was all-too-easy for the home side to play through Liverpool. For the seventh goal (ugh), John McGinn was able to play Jack Grealish clean through on goal when both players were still inside the Villa half.

There was a circle of six Liverpool players who were all equidistant from McGinn, and as that distance could've been classified as 'a long bloody way', there was clearly a problem. That would've been true wherever the last man in the defence happened to be stationed at that point.

What happened at Villa Park was extreme in every sense. It brought to mind a recent comment I posted on TTT a while back though, which showed that Liverpool's pressing had dropped off after they had won the title. Could they switch it back on when truly competitive football began again for them for the first time in over six months when 2020/21 began? And more pertinently, is there any correlation between the Reds not pressing as well and getting worse results? Let's see.

The sample sizes are wildly different, but Liverpool's pressing success average is the lowest for losses (28.8%), then better for draws (30.7%) and best of all for victories (31.6%), which stands to reason. There appears to be a sweet spot for a one goal win – where the success rate is 32.1% – but of course such matches are also the most intense. It makes sense that the pressing success would tail off a little when the team is three-or-more goals up, for instance, though the Reds are still successful with 31.3% of their pressures in matches won by that margin.

However, not all of the findings make logical sense. *Statsbomb* have a metric for passes made under pressure from an opponent. Teams facing Liverpool attempt a lower proportion of their passes when pressured by the Red wave when they lose rather than when they take something from the match. You'd assume Klopp's team would press passers more often in victories, but on this evidence that is not the case.

In the last three full seasons, 17.2% of passes in the Premier League were made while being pressed. For Liverpool's collective opponents, this figure is 19.2%. Marginal gains right there, folks. Yet when looking at the 119 league games between Mohamed Salah's debut at Vicarage Road and the recent Merseyside derby, the 7-2 defeat at Villa was ranked 25th for the *highest* proportion of opposition passes made under Red pressure. The aforementioned moment with McGinn was clearly not one of them, and it's a very surprising discovery that – by this measure at least – the debacle in the west Midlands would be considered a good pressing performance. Dean Smith's side were also allowed fewer touches per Liverpool pressure than average over the last three years, and that applies across the whole field, but also in their defensive and midfield thirds specifically. Only in their attacking third did they get more touches per press than average, and even then their figure of 2.8 isn't much above the standard rate of 2.6.

And as ever with Liverpool, it's hard not to suspect that there's a deeper plan at play than can be unpicked by the naked eye. We must be wary of small samples, but the data is sure to make you think. Don't you wonder some time?

Liverpool's pressing fell off a cliff after Project Restart in June, which was to be expected. The league was all-but-won for the first two matches, then definitely in the bag for the final seven of the 2019/20 campaign.

But what strikes me as interesting is that they are not pressing opposition passers as frequently – the rate was 21.2% pre-lockdown in 2019/20 and has been 19% this season – nor quite as often, but the success rate has gone up. The proportion of successful presses (which are those where possession is regained within five seconds) is higher than in any past campaign in the early days of 2020/21, at 32.8%, and even higher since the restart (33.5%).

There have been 294 team seasons in Europe's big five leagues in the last three years, and only three of them – two for Bayern Munich, one for Bayer Leverkusen – have seen a team record a higher pressing success rate than the Reds have logged since football went behind closed doors. Even their rate for this season alone (all five games of it, granted) would be the fifth best in a sample of almost 300.

Perhaps we're seeing the early days of the latest pressing evolution at Liverpool? Maybe what happened against Aston Villa was an acute demonstration of the flaws with the new system? Perhaps the sample is too small and the averages will return to normal over the next few months? And maybe the long-term unavailability of van Dijk will force a tactical tweak to render any theoretical new tactical plan moot in any case?

Who knows? 'Not I', said the Walrus. But whatever the truth of it, there's clearly more to what's happening than a high line in isolation. The next step will be to see if this is truly intentional, or whether it will be filed under 'weird stuff which happened during behind-closed-doors football'. Either way, the hope has to be that it doesn't affect the pressing at the front end of the team. It was potent enough to make Liverpool the *champions of everywhere*.

The Toxic Rot of the Unhappy Superstar And How It's Not An Issue For Klopp's Liverpool

By Paul Tomkins

September 30th 2020

The thing that many fans don't seem to understand about superstars is the all-consuming vibe-drain that occurs when they become unhappy. A struggling side with an unhappy superstar is perhaps worse than a struggling side with inferior talent.

The superstar is often great when things are on the up, although even then, he may cause problems: is he a dickhead who flouts club rules, and gets preferential treatment, or is paid disproportionately high wages? Does he put in a shift on the pitch, or leave that to everyone else? How does team unity function when there's a diva around? Is it right that some players disappear for Carnival every year? But Jürgen Klopp and Michael Edwards have steered their way around this problem, by not signing superstars and by not signing dickheads.

(And 'dickheads', within football terminology, need not *necessarily* mean bad or egotistical people, as it also includes those who just can never make it to training or team meetings on time, even if they are being paid £300,000 a week and could presumably afford a coterie of people to physically lift them out of bed, carry them into their Ferrari and drive them to the training ground on time.)

So, superstars need not be dickheads – many of the best are often elite professionals, albeit some get caught up in their own hype and the fawning of their entourage. But they can clearly be problematic, and toxic. I cover this toxicity in a chapter in

Perched: Jürgen Klopp's Liverpool FC – Champions Of Everything, although I can take it one step further here.

As Manchester City, at home to Leicester, suffered their 10th league defeat in less than a season's worth of games, it reminded me of other teams who had sulking superstars pouting and pointing on the pitch as the ship goes down. And it struck me about how Liverpool, on numerous levels, have almost immunised themselves from such a problem.

Sam Lee, the Manchester City correspondent for *The Athletic*, writing after Leicester came from behind to humiliate City at the Etihad with a 5-2 win, said that:

"The worst thing about Manchester City's collapse is that they have done all this before. When they were knocked out of the Champions League by Lyon not that long ago, Kevin De Bruyne declared it 'different year, same stuff', and it looks like not much has changed since then.

"… But as De Bruyne — not entirely blameless himself — spent the second half on Sunday shouting at half his team (Phil Foden about where to position himself in midfield, Rodri about where to stand in the wall and [Eric] Garcia for his role in Vardy's impudent second) it really did feel like different year, same stuff. And they will not learn."

This reminded me a bit of the sullen-faced Steven Gerrard in many of the seasons after 2009, or the moody Lionel Messi of the past two years, seeing their teams get humped, and somehow adding to the bad vibes with their body language and scowling disapprovals. It's not even that they don't care; perhaps they care too much.

The more the team is built around one player, the more damage is done when both they and the team cannot get into their grooves. The superstar may themselves feel more pressure, as the talisman, and may beat themselves up even more than they metaphorically beat up their teammates.

When your go-to player looks gone, but still starts every week, it's game up. They appear impotent and full of rage and frustration, and the more they take it out on their teammates or moan in the media, the more the anxiety levels creep up. It often takes a new manager to allow a release of tension, and the belief that something new can be done about it – but of course, the release of pressure may just be temporary, as a new pressure begins to build.

When the superstar's powers are in permanent decline – when they melt (albeit rarely without an Indian summer or two) – then you are stuck playing a myth as a false nine or a creative midfielder; or a sluggish leader unable to chase back anymore.

City are not yet at that stage with Kevin de Bruyne, but he must be doing what Gerrard and Jamie Carragher did at Liverpool, and Lionel Messi did at Barcelona, and look with despair and perhaps even disdain at the club's recruitment (albeit the superstar is obviously never going to be happy if the recruitment is perfect enough to render *them* obsolete; it's always someone else who needs replacing – and if the manager is looking to ship them out then suddenly it's the manager who must go). The team de Bruyne joined had Sergio Agüero, Vincent Kompany, David Silva, Yaya Touré and Fernandinho, and coincided with the arrival of Raheem Sterling.

They were miles ahead of Liverpool, and better in every department. They added Ederson, and Leroy Sané, plus the still-improving Gabriel Jesus, as well as the hot-and-cold Kyle Walker and strangely deteriorated (lately) and increasingly narky Bernardo Silva, but otherwise spent hundreds of millions on defensive duds and unremarkable midfielders, and some decent squad players at best. They still have a ton of good players, but not many *great* ones; and right now, not a lot of unity and desire. Maybe that will change, but the vibes don't look too good. Unhappy teams full of division can still succeed, but it seems much rarer.

Now, it looks like only de Bruyne would get in the Liverpool side, with Roberto Firmino a much better all-round player and more reliable than the ageing Agüero, and Sterling definitely no better than Mo Salah or Sadio Mané – even before you even take into account the collective brilliance of the Reds' famous trident, where they exceed the sum of their parts.

You could argue that Sterling is younger, therefore a better option; but the same logic would then take perhaps the only other City option to stand a chance of getting in the Liverpool XI – Aymeric Laporte as partner to Virgil van Dijk – and counter his inclusion with the fact that Joe Gomez, at just 23, is not even close to his prime yet, and should only improve [note: this was written when Liverpool's best defenders still had *knees*]. Even Fabinho looks capable of being a world-class centre-back, as I've been saying for almost two years, given his physique and skillset. Liverpool might take the City man if he was available, but they don't *need* Laporte.

Even allowing for my own bias, I know that I would have loved to take most of the City side of a few years ago, and right now none of them interest me. Even de Bruyne seems less necessary when you've just won the league with 99 points and added Thiago Alcântara.

Maybe a generous neutral might select three or four City players in a mixed XI, but even that would be an incredible switch from the early months of 2017/18, when most neutrals would probably have picked the entire City side. Again, these things can change with form, and perceptions can swiftly alter, but Fernandinho and Agüero are not going to get younger and fitter.

How Klopp Works Without Superstars

The difference between world-class managers and world-class players is usually that the manager is older, wiser, and less egotistical. Now, there are exceptions, but the manager is clearly supposed to be the adult in the room. He is the one who, more than anyone else, has to take responsibility for results, and as such, it's in his interests to park his ego.

Many great managers have big egos, but they know they have to blend together a team of younger men, with egos of their own. Unless the manager's aura is all about projecting a godlike ego (early Jose Mourinho, before he morphed into carrying the look of a drug-addled bin-man), the need is usually to keep it in check. If the manager makes it all about himself, then he *really* has to be special.

Big personalities also usually mean big egos; but with Jürgen Klopp that's just not the case. Smaller managers – "little men" – would try to increase their chances of "success" by redefining failure, so that falling short becomes exceeding targets.

Klopp is carrying the weight of a massive club, with huge expectations, and yet he has only served to *raise* expectations, and smile in the process. Contrast that to the manager the current owners inherited a decade ago – Roy Hodgson – who was looking to laud even potential mid-table finishes as an achievement; and who at least twice stated how eager he was that his Liverpool team didn't lose 6-0 (one of which was in a preseason game against an obscure Middle Eastern side); and so when his side only lost 3-0, as it did in his second league game (at Manchester

City, prior to their rise to dominance), it was a big achievement. The weight of the job seemed to crush Hodgson within weeks, just as David Moyes was almost immediately squashed by the scale of the job at Manchester United (although apparently his face has always looked that way).

People have accused Klopp of somehow faking his personality (some odious "nice bloke syndrome" comment a year or so ago on a podcast springs to mind, where he was compared with a load of largely talentless personalities whom those talking clearly hated: Jamie Oliver, James Corden, et al). Sadly, I think some people still don't get how genuinely authentic Klopp is, in an era of fake-it-till-you-make-it, and never-ending PR guff about keeping it real. After all, authenticity is what everyone learns to fake. He wears his heart on his sleeve, and means what he says; with a mix of his religious beliefs and a kind of ancient Stoic wisdom that predates Christianity.

Klopp is both positive *and* realistic. He never sought to sell false dreams, and when he said titles could be delivered within five years he was right. Progress to that point was never over-sold, nor undercut. He praised the team without ever making it sound like finishing 4th or losing a Champions League final was enough; but he made it clear that the process had been fun, and that success would arrive with a mixture of hard work and living in the moment. Training would be intense, but never boring.

It takes a big personality to do what he's done, especially on a budget that is well short of the average spending of title winners, having inherited a mediocre squad (so it's not like he won the league with a team that had recently done so), with some talented players having left, retired or found themselves crippled by injuries. He took on a defence and goalkeeper that was punch drunk, and a side that could not score goals. The midfield wasn't up to much, either. Almost no one would remain very long, and those who did had to improve.

Then you have the lower-ego managers who are low-key – the quiet thinkers, the gentlemen, the studious and largely keep-it-calm brigade: Pep Guardiola, Arsène Wenger, Rafa Benítez, Carlo Ancelotti, and purely as he's a bit different to other English managers and wears a waistcoat, Gareth Southgate. They are quiet leaders, whose egos are largely in-check, albeit perhaps still prone to demonstrative behaviour. Perhaps you could argue that someone like Guardiola has an *enormous* ego, especially as his team is built in his image and who demands subservient players, but his aura is more about being a thinker. Of course, to some observers, Klopp's gregarious nature obscures his own clear intelligence, and sees him caricatured as a ranting motivator. Klopp feels far closer to Guardiola on tactical issues than Guardiola feels to Klopp on interpersonal skills. Pep is so intense that I fear I'd get a migraine just saying hello to him.

In truth, *no one* is like Jürgen Klopp. I'm not sure anyone in football management history has mixed the hugeness of personality and physique – which I don't think is inconsequential – with the smallness of ego, and an exacting, scientific attention to detail. Few top managers have had so little ego that they bring in all manner of experts, and openly admit that the experts know more, which is why they were hired. Klopp was never a great footballer, so that helped keep him humble; but he was always a big man, and therefore always a physical presence, which meant he was neither a shrinking violet, nor could he therefore possess a Napoleon complex.

By contrast, Brendan Rodgers' ego – or maybe, more fairly, his massive insecurities (which some might compare to Klopp in terms of their contrasting physical stature) – see him talk about himself too much, pointing out every clever idea he himself has had (a real douche move, albeit I've one I've also been known to pull, which, by admitting it, *is showing just how human I am*, and is therefore in itself a humble brag that's all about me. Result!).

With Klopp, it's all about *us*.

Klopp is 6'4" of manic Teutonic teeth and eyes and spectacle lenses, and he can both be raging taskmaster and a beaming comic, switching from genuine fuming fury to friendly and Zen, but authentically, *in the moment*; not to grandstand or self-aggrandise. He doesn't need to tell the world, as Rodgers did at the weekend at some length, how clever his own tactics were (such speeches were strangely absent when Leicester nosedived from title contenders to finishing outside the top four in 2020). Klopp is utterly self-secure.

Then, as a consequence, the relationship this absolutely unique manager has to his players is in itself an ego-buster. He is almost too big, both physically and as a character – but also boosted by his body of work, his *cachet* – to be undermined by the players. That he doesn't make it all about him only further inoculates him from sedition. The players are never bigger than the manager, and no one arrives on superstar wages; and even the best players have to earn their bonuses. No one is too big for a bollocking.

Maybe there's a bit of Alex Ferguson about Klopp in this regard – in that Ferguson built such a power base at his club, where no one dare go against his wishes or they'd get a boot in their face or shipped off to Italy or Spain. I wanted to add that no one dares *question* Klopp, but it feels like he'd actually be open to being debated on any given issue by his players, such is the trust, and such is his own security. He would not automatically cede to their wishes just to have them like him more, but he'd take them seriously; more so than someone like Brian Clough, who once admitted that whenever he faced dissent from the ranks he'd let the player give his side, as if it was a fair-minded debate, before the dissenter was forced to agree that he, *the manager*, was right all along.

That old authoritarianism, also personified by Bill Shankly, is probably impossible in the modern game, with players holding so much power. It's probably still partially possible with a group of plucky underdogs who feel lucky just to be in the Premier League (so you could run your own personal fiefdom at Burnley or Sheffield United), but's impossible with so many famous players whose agents, publicists, extended families and entourages all feel like they too have a say in club matters, like in-laws who think they have an equal say in a relative's marriage.

Just witness the nonsense that surrounded a mere U18 player wanting out of Liverpool in 2019 despite having signed a contract and been progressing steadily through the age groups; a player who went to Italy, failed, and is now part of Derby County's youth setup. Bobby Duncan has since admitted the error of his ways, or the ways of those representing him, but it was a case of superstar diva behaviour – conducted via Twitter – from his adviser, for a player who had zero professional games under his belt. His agent mocked Michael Edwards, as if Edwards wasn't a big factor in Liverpool being champions of Europe at the time, and as if he, Saif Rubie, had achieved anything of note in the sport. Duncan has since ditched Rubie, who was fined and suspended by the FA for his part in the debacle, but not before the player's fledgeling Liverpool career was torpedoed.

Imagine if any senior players thought they could get away with any of that shit. Part of the problem is avoided by not signing dickheads, but it's also the total respect the manager commands.

So a manager needs to be both an authority figure, but one with a human side. However, get the balance wrong, and players will start to take advantage – if "too soft" they will get slack and breach rules, ease off in training. On the pitch, they will crawl into their proverbial shells with fear if he is too strict, or just feel unloved and disconnected, especially if not a regular starter.

In recent years the concept of bullying within sport has really taken hold, yet the carrot and the stick were alway the two ways to lead; now, the stick is often equated with psychological abuse.

Indeed, this was the case Rubie made against Edwards, because Edwards would not grant him and his client a free transfer, not least as he was under contract. More and more of life (and working life) is seen through the lens of power dynamics. By its very definition, sports have to have hierarchies; there must be bosses, and leaders, who give instructions to others to follow. Players sign contracts to be "owned"; and that contract protects them when they are not in the team (or seriously injured), but are still earning their salary.

Alex Ferguson was also allowed to rule with fear, in a different era, as just one more advantage he had in keeping power at Old Trafford. Even if he wanted to, Klopp cannot pull the same power tricks – but he can be about as authoritative as it's possible to be in 2020. And he retains that authority in part as players don't seem to tire of him, in part due to his rounded personality.

Like Ferguson, Klopp *is* the superstar. He is Liverpool's biggest name, its key man. He is unique, and uniquely brilliant, and the way he unites the disparate group of races, nationalities and religions who form the squad is itself a beautiful modern parable. That unprecedented success has followed is the icing on the cake.

Master Oogway's Wise Words

Comment on TTT By Mobykidz

October 5th (the day after Liverpool lost 7-2 at Aston Villa)

It's 5am. I wrote something but my phone crashed and I lost the post. It's quiet now. All I can hear is the humming of my satellite box as it updates itself thinking I'd be asleep. I can hear the rain and where my gutter has split a stream of water lashes my window. I need to replace that tomorrow as every time it rains it feels worse than it really is. It's not urgent or doing any long term damage. Just really annoying right now.

I have to wake up in a couple of hours and take the kids to school. One is a Liverpool fan and the other a Gooner. I feel sorry for him as his twin brother will be gleeful. It's like Watford but statistically x2.5 times worse – but x25 worse in emotional terms. Come the end of the game both said goodnight being school tomorrow, which is now today. Both said it quietly. They knew the result and each for their own reasons didn't want to talk.

I never bashed my virtual or real keyboards last night. There was no pent up anger or emotions flying around. I sat there quiet and when my other half came in my only request was to let me just be. I needed an hour to write something, to let my PC run its update and in general to wind down my evening.

As I watched the software update run from 1% to 100% in just over 10 minutes I felt calmer – an excuse not to write more. So I switched the upstairs light off and checked the kids were sleeping.

I bought them an Emma mattress each so whatever happens during the day they will have a decent sleep at night. Whatever stress getting a good night's sleep is a must. So splashing out on a good mattress feels like a wise investment even though it takes a little bit of getting used to as it moulds around your form. The good thing is you have a 200 nights return guarantee after purchase. But after getting one I've been sleeping really comfortably for the past 80 nights. So one lost night ain't going to change that. But I still need to fix that guttering.

How am I going to feel tomorrow now that tomorrow is today? In actual fact the same. The gutters need fixing. I need to make a wardrobe so my kids can hang up their stuff instead of using a cheap rail. I need to take the car in to check the brakes and go out and get some groceries. Plus get that gutter looked at. Nothing special. Just the usual stuff. That's our routine – it doesn't change because these things need to get done.

It's 5am. And I don't feel stressed. I am not reading the news, obituaries or any other content. Netflix will be my companion today. I have already identified a bit of binge watching.

It's 10.30pm last night. There goes my WhatsApp notification. It's my Gooner brother saying "Ha Ha It's all falling apart". Do I reply? So I draft "LOL but we are still level in points" and then I add "hope mum is feeling better, she didn't sound too great ..." to which he responds "she is :-)". This lockdown has been awful. She can't go out. She is ill but I'm thankful that my big Gooner brother is there with them. We can't visit any more and my boys are upset. There are just more important things in life for a 13-year-old.

I think my satellite box has updated. The rain has stopped. This mattress is really comfortable. But I can't go to sleep. Not because of... My mind is focused on tomorrow which is now today. Call mum, find a roofer, make that furniture and take the car to the garage. First thing in the morning my task list is set.

When the kids wake up in under two hours I will help them get ready for school. We will talk about what happened last night and I will shrug my shoulders and say nothing is perfect in life and sometimes however much we plan things can go wrong. And we need to accept and learn from that because after all it's only a game. Even after those 90 minutes are over there's still a wardrobe to make, a gutter to fix, a car to repair, school run to make, and so on. Life goes on and we treat Yesterday as history, Tomorrow as a mystery, And Today as a gift ... that's why they call it the present!

These are the wise words courtesy of Master Oogway and my kids' favourite movie – Kung Fu Panda. I wonder if Netflix has it?

How To Recognise The Start Of Decline And How To Avoid It

By Bob Pearce
October 5th

As the 2019/20 season finally reached a conclusion, Liverpool FC stood on top of the world with arguably the best playing squad, coaching and recruitment staff, and administrators and ownership in the world.

As the 2020/21 season begins, fans and pundits will begin to speculate about whether Liverpool FC have reached the peak (speculation that could only be enhanced by that defeat at Villa

Park). Will they maintain their superiority? Could they continue to ascend to higher peaks? Or will we see them descend to rejoin what had been a distant chasing pack? My mate will say, social media will reckon, ex-players will suggest and journalists will explain.

So how would you know?

Some will simply judge from one result to the next. So how would you know intuition from outrage? Some could look past the results and judge from one performance to the next. So how would you know a mystic from a neurotic? Some could look past the results and performances, and judge from one big data trend to the next. So how would you know a blip from a dip?

It is not my intention to go drizzling on anybody's parade here. I'm looking for some reliable indicators that would help us to distinguish between some click baiting 'wolf'-crying boy and an actual big bad wolf, with big scary teeth.

So how would you know? I'm not looking for a reassuring answer today, that could be worthless tomorrow. I want us to be asking more reassuring questions. I want to start a different conversation that may be a more reliable way for us to judge where Liverpool FC stand today, tomorrow, next week, next season, and for seasons to come.

Jim Collins is the author of international best sellers *'Good to Great'* and *'Built to Last'*, and has featured in *Fortune, BusinessWeek, The Economist, USA Today,* and *Harvard Business Review.* In 2004 he was invited to West Point by the Leader to Leader Institute to lead a discussion.

"At the break, the chief executive of one of America's most successful companies pulled me aside." he remembered. "He mused, 'We've had tremendous success in recent years, and I worry about that. When you are at the top of the world, the most powerful nation on Earth, the most successful company in your industry, the best player in your game, your very power and success might cover up the fact that you're already on the path to decline. So how would you know?'."

That seemed to me to be a more helpful question to ask.

As Collins put it:

"Great enterprises can become insulated by success; accumulated momentum can carry an enterprise forward, for a while, even if its leaders make poor decisions or lose discipline." He wondered "Might it be possible to detect decline early and reverse course, or even better, might we be able to practice preventative medicine?"

He spent four years looking for answers to this question. He shared his findings in his 2009 book *'How The Mighty Fall'*.

"I've come to see institutional decline like a staged disease" he concluded. "Harder to detect but easier to cure in the early stages, easier to detect but harder to cure in the later stages. An institution can look strong on the outside but already be sick on the inside, dangerously on the cusp of a precipitous fall ... and that can make the process of decline so terrifying; it can sneak up on you, and then – seemingly all of a sudden – you're in big trouble."

Collins was studying the world of business but maybe his findings could be applied to the business of football.

While some pick over results, performances and data, they may be missing something right under their noses. We can reassure ourselves by saying the results are going our way, we're doing just fine, nothing to worry about here. What happens to that reassurance when results don't go our way? Wouldn't it be more reassuring to be having a regular diagnostic 'MOT' to check and detect making it easier to spot and stop any worries before they build up a momentum of doom? Wouldn't it be more reassuring to be able to enjoy the good results and endure the bad results while knowing we have a clean bill of health and we're in good shape?

Collins' research found a pattern of five step-wise stages of decline and identified a collection of 'markers' for each stage. I'm asking if we could use these 'markers' as that diagnostic tool. Like a doctor analysing test results, Collins stresses that:

"Not every marker shows up in every case of decline, and the presence of a marker does not necessarily mean that you have a disease.", but, he warned, "It does indicate an increased possibility that you're in that stage of decline."

I'm very aware that this discussion has the potential to grow into a very long article. To keep it manageable I will not go into great detail on all five stages. Today we're looking for what may be indicators of the early stages of decline. So I'll focus on stages one and two and glance over at stages three, four and five, way off over there in the distance. To also keep this article digestible, I want to resist the temptation to stop every few sentences to point out evidence of where the model seems to be helpful. I'll leave you to bring forward your examples of evidence from within the club today, to judge the value of the model and what it may tell us about the health of Liverpool FC (and I mean the whole club, from the playing squad, through to the coaching and recruiting staff, and the administration and ownership).

Collins called Stage 1 'Hubris Born On Success':

"Like an artist who pursues both enduring excellence *and* shocking creativity, great companies foster a productive tension between continuity *and* change …. When institutions fail to distinguish between current practices and the enduring principles of success, and mistakenly fossilise around their practices, they've set themselves up for decline …. The point here is not as simple as 'they failed because they didn't change' …. Companies that change but without any consistent rationale will collapse just as surely as those that change not at all. There's nothing inherently wrong with adhering to specific practices and strategies (indeed, we see tremendous consistency over time in great companies), but only if you comprehend the underlying *why* behind those practices, and thereby see when to keep them and when to change them."

There were five 'markers' that Collins suggested were an indication of 'Hubris Born On Success':

Success entitlement, arrogance:

"Success is viewed as 'deserved', rather than fortuitous, fleeting, or even hard-earned in the face of daunting odds; people begin to believe that success will continue almost no matter what the organisation decides to do, or not to do."

Neglect of a primary flywheel:

"Distracted by extraneous threats, adventures, and opportunities, leaders neglect a primary flywheel, failing to renew it with the same creative intensity that made it great in the first place."

'What' replaces 'why':

"The rhetoric of success ('We're successful because we do these specific things') replaces penetrating understanding and insight ('We're successful because we *understand* why we do these specific things and under what conditions they would no longer work')."

Decline in learning orientation:

"Leaders lose the inquisitiveness and learning orientation that marks those truly great individuals who, no matter how successful they become, maintain a learning curve as steep as when they first began their careers."

Discounting the role of luck:

"Instead of acknowledging that luck and fortuitous events might have played a helpful role, people begin to presume that success is due entirely to the superior qualities of the enterprise and its leadership."

I'm going to suggest that you just pause for a moment now and think about those five diagnostic 'markers' of 'Hubris Born On Success'. As you currently look around Liverpool FC, do you see evidence of any of these 'markers' within the playing squad, the coaching and recruiting staff, and the administration and ownership today? If not, that should be a huge reassurance whenever results, performances and data do not look so well today, tomorrow, next week, next season and for seasons to come.

If you do see evidence of these 'markers' appearing within the club, it will not be conclusive but, to repeat, "It does indicate an increased possibility that you're in that stage of decline." This model should also give reassurance that, even if results, performances and data were looking good you could keep a close eye on those 'markers' and you'd want to look out for evidence of the next stage, which Collins called *'Undisciplined Pursuit of More'*.

"If a great company consistently grows revenues faster than its ability to get enough of the right people to implement that growth, it will not simply stagnate; it will fall." he explained. "Any exceptional enterprise depends first and foremost upon having self-managed and self-motivated people – the #1 ingredient for a culture of discipline .... One notable distinction between wrong people and right people is that the former see themselves as having 'jobs', while the latter see themselves as having *responsibilities*. Every person in a key seat should be able to respond to the question 'What do you do?' *not* with a job title, but with a statement of personal responsibility."

Collins suggests there are seven 'markers' that could indicate 'Undisciplined Pursuit of More'.

"Unsustainable quest for growth, confusing big with growth:

Success creates pressure for more growth, setting up a vicious cycle of expectations; this strains people, the culture, and the systems to the breaking point; unable to deliver consistent tactical excellence, the institution frays at the edges.

Undisciplined discontinuous leaps:

The enterprise makes dramatic moves that fail at least one of the three tests: 1. Do they ignite passion and fit with the company's core values? 2. Can the organisation be the best in the world at these activities or in these arenas? 3. Will these activities help drive the organisation's economic or resource engine?

Declining proportion of right people in key seats:

There is a declining proportion of right people in key seats, because of losing the right people and/or growing beyond the organisation's ability to get enough people to execute on that growth with excellence.

Easy cash erodes cost discipline:

The organisation responds to increasing costs by increasing prices and revenues rather than increasing discipline.

Bureaucracy subverts discipline:

A system of bureaucratic rules subverts the ethic of freedom and responsibility that marks a culture of discipline; people increasingly think in terms of 'jobs' rather than *responsibilities*.

Problematic succession of power:

The organisation experiences leadership-transition difficulties, be they in the form of poor succession planning, failure to groom excellent leaders from within, political turmoil, bad luck, or an unwise selection of successors.

Personal interest placed above organisational interests:

People in power allocate more for themselves or their constituents – more money, more privileges, more fame, more of the spoils of success – seeking to capitalise as much as possible in the short term, rather than investing primarily in building for greatness decades into the future."

"If I were to pick one marker above all others to use as a warning sign," Collins concluded "it would be a declining proportion of key seats filled with the right people .... What are your backup plans in the event that a right person leaves a key seat? .... In all but one case in our analysis of decline, we observed signs of a problematic succession of power by the end of Stage 2 .... Leaders who fail the process of succession set their enterprises on a path of decline .... The evidence leads me to this sobering conclusion: while no leader can single-handedly build an enduring great company, the wrong leader vested with power can almost single-handedly bring a company down .... From what we've seen in this study, Stage 2 overreaching tends to increase after a legendary leader steps way .... Whatever the underlying dynamic, when companies engage in Stage 2 overreaching *and* bungle the transfer of power, they tend to hurtle towards Stage 3 and beyond."

I'd suggest that you pause again here for a moment to think about those seven diagnostic 'markers' of 'Undisciplined Pursuit of More' that we could be looking out for within the playing squad, the coaching and recruiting staff, and the administration and ownership of Liverpool FC today.

To briefly sketch out the remaining stages of the momentum of decline, Collins explains that:

"As companies move into Stage 3, we begin to see the cumulative effects of the previous stages. Stage 1 hubris leads to Stage 2 overreaching, which sets the company up for Stage 3, *Denial of Risk and Peril* .... Leaders discount negative data, amplify positive data, and put a positive spin on ambiguous data .... The vigorous, fact-based dialogue that characterises high-performance teams dwindles or disappears altogether."

He described the fourth stage as *Grasping for Salvation*, which "Begins when an organisation reacts to a downturn by lurching for a silver bullet .... they go for a quick, big solution or bold stroke to jump-start a recovery, rather than embark on the more pedestrian, arduous process of rebuilding long-term momentum."

Collins described the final fifth stage as *Capitulation to Irrelevance or Death*:

"As institutions hurtle towards Stage 5, they spiral downward, increasingly out of control. Each cycle – grasping followed by disappointment followed by more grasping – erodes resources. Cash tightens. Hope fades. Options narrow."

'How The Mighty Fall' seems like a model that can help us to go beyond the intuition and outrage, the mystic and neurotic, and the blips and dips of results, performances and data, to provide a diagnostic of Liverpool FC that offers both the reassurance of good health, and the reassurance of early detection of health concerns. It seems like a model that can be used today, tomorrow, next week, next season and for seasons to come.

Before finishing, it's worth saying that there will be many other ways to use this model to look at the business of football. Could it help us understand what may have happened at Liverpool FC in the 30 years between league titles. 'How the

Mighty Fall' tells us that "By understanding these stages of decline, leaders can substantially reduce their chances of falling all the way to the bottom." And when Liverpool FC were at the High Court in October 2010 we all got a terrifyingly close look at what 'the bottom' looks like. We could ask if that day in Liverpool FC's history was a culmination of the five stages of 'How the Mighty Fall'.

Collins also tells us that:

"Every institution, no matter how great, is vulnerable to decline. There is no law of nature that the most powerful will inevitably remain at the top. Anyone can fall and most eventually do."

But, as his research emphasises, some companies do indeed recover – in some cases, coming back stronger – even after having crashed into the depths of Stage 4." He tells us:

"Decline can be avoided. Decline can be detected. Decline can be reversed."

The past decade at Liverpool FC, under new ownership, has shown that "An alternative to Stage 5 can be Recovery and Renewal," as Collins reported. "Our research indicates that organisational decline is largely self inflicted, and recovery largely within our own control."

Another possible use for the 'How the Mighty Fall' model may be as a diagnostic to speculate which stage other rival 'Top 6' clubs, and even 'Mid 6' clubs, have come from, where they stand today, and where they seem to be headed.

Instead of 'my mate saying', social media reckoning, ex-players suggesting and journalists explaining, 'How the Mighty Fall' may be a model that can give us a reassuring way to look for answers to the question *So how would you know?'*

Football 2020: Amusing Ourselves to Death

By Daniel Rhodes

The very fact you are reading a book is progress (*put that Kindle down and buy the real thing*). Screens dominate life and attention spans, and are often the only vehicles of social interaction we have anymore, especially since the emergence of SARS Covid-2. In fact, on average, we look at our phones four times an hour. And four hours in total. Every single day. Though that still seems on the low side.

Working for *The Tomkins Times*, I check the website at least that many times an hour. This means I'm thinking about Liverpool Football Club in one way or another fifty-two times a day (*assuming I'm awake for around sixteen hours, though it's often more*). Again, that figure seems on the low side and needs some work! How many times do you think about our beloved club every twenty-four hours?

The reason I'm posing this question is because, having recently watched *The Social Dilemma* – the Netflix documentary seen by 38 million households in the first 28 days about social media and manipulation – it made me think about how we are engaging with the world around us. And also the changing dynamic we have in the relationship with football, our football club, and more specifically the football matches.

Liverpool are the current Premier League Champions, and we still haven't celebrated. Of course we have, in our own ways, but not together. No fans to scream, shout, sing and smile as we beat Chelsea and lifted the trophy. Great fireworks. Life-lasting iconic images. But, after all those years, all that waiting, all that heartache, we didn't even get to fucking celebrate it together. No parade with – possibly – over a million fans lining the streets. Celebrating together. We can't all get tickets, but those of us lucky enough to live close enough to visit the city had been looking forward to that moment for thirty years. That's 946,080,000 seconds. Or the number of aerial duels Virgil van Dijk won last season. Those players, who basically won the league dropping only two points (*by the time the Reds lost to Watford it was already over, and then some*), haven't had any songs sung in the Kop yet. *You'll Never Walk Alone* as champions. They've not had that yet. We've not either. They haven't been adored by the adoring fans.

We've still got that to come ....

What have we got at the moment though? It doesn't feel like Football 2019. We can hear the players shouting at each other on the pitch. We heard Frank Lampard acting like a dickhead. We can hear Jordan Henderson conducting. Or, depressingly, we get fake crowd noise. Often badly-timed, it's like watching a film when the audio is not in sync with the images. Football has got to the stage where it has to exist, because without the money from the broadcasters, most clubs in the Premier League would probably go under. Football has got to the stage where it *can* exist without fans. Football has got to the stage where *it only* exists on the screen. Liverpool won the league on the screen. Thankfully, more meaning attaches to that song from the Anfield crowd – after beating Man United last season – with every passing week. Liverpool had *already* won the league. We had already started the long celebration. The longest procession in English footballing history.

How did football get to this position though, and is it healthy? One quote, from an editorial on '*Game Of the People*' blog, outlines what football is – and on its historical popularity:

"A chin-stroking professor, trying to explain the typical extra-curricular activities of British people, once remarked that in any group of 100 men, around 50% spent much of their free time watching 'association' football. He went on to explain that for many of these people, the game of football was, to a certain degree, the replacement for some of the conventional life-defining moments that people live through. Invariably, the nationwide obsession for a game that owed its commercial origins in Victorian England, has instilled a devotion to every intrinsic detail of its history, its protagonists and its execution. For 90 minutes, the followers of football teams are so transfixed, so blinkered in their support of their favourites, that nothing else matters while a game is in progress."

When, as a fan, you have such an emotional investment, then the ability of *any* club to 'exploit' that for financial gain is just about the easiest pound to take, other than maybe the ability of the pub landlord. Whether individual clubs do or not is another story, but the dynamic has now changed. It feels like broadcasters are the ones in control. Without their 'investment', which is just another funnel of finance to fans' pockets, football clubs (before Covid) who were in healthy financial positions, would cease to exist because of the reliance on broadcasting revenue as a ratio of total revenue. Premier League football can now exist without fans in the stadium because of this dependency on broadcasting revenue. Of course, that depends solely on football fans continuing to buy TV subscriptions and pay-per-view matches. And, as far as is public knowledge, they do continue to do so (even if certain objections were made to the PPV, but we'll come back to that later).

Is sport now just entertainment? On-screen entertainment, designed to amuse us? Like Netflix, YouTube and social media? David Goldblatt wrote about this in *The Guardian*, again before the pandemic, in 2018:

"Fortunate as we are to have such an accurate avatar of our lives, it makes me wonder whether football's uncanny capacity to reflect our social identities and collective moods is also a curse. Many of us, myself included, still look to football as an entertainment, a glorious illusion, a soap opera of distraction. Even though we all know that the spectacle is deformed by the worlds of commerce and politics, we still want to disappear into the zone of play, pleasure and irrelevance: at the game, on the screen, lost in our noisy Twitter feeds. But this season, reality just keeps on intruding, and I don't want to look."

He continues:

"...the situation at West Ham is just one of dozens of conflicts between fans and owners. However, what gives it real edge and momentum is that the move from the club's old East End stadium – sold off for high-end housing – to the Olympic Stadium (a £200m subsidy to West Ham Plc) has been an emotional and experiential disaster: soulless, fragmented, deracinated and anodyne. In the absence of any kind of real voice, and with the option of exit blocked by emotional loyalties, a part of the fan base has turned to intimidation and riot."

Going back even further to September 2011, Rory Smith wrote 'Is Football Still Sport' in *The Blizzard*:

"March 9th this year, the morning after Barcelona, at their impish, dervish best, had exhilarated in excoriating Arsenal in the Champions League. For the 90 minutes of that 3-1 second leg win, sport happened, sport at its absolute best, two teams of impeccable technical expertise – though, in truth, substantially better – seeking glory.

"The headlines the next day? 'Referee killed us, insists Wenger,' read *The Times*, in reference to Massimo Busacca's officious – but hardly criminally baffling – decision to dismiss Robin van Persie minutes into the second half. The beauty of Barcelona was relegated to second billing behind the whisper of illusory controversy. The latest instalment is all that matters. That's enough of the sport, let's get back to the story.

"Everything, in football, is heightened. Reality is not enough, so it is expanded, meaning is extrapolated, significance is assumed. And all of it around a structure to ensure maximum exposure, maximum interest, to guarantee, as [Neal] Gabler puts it, that its characters fulfil their contracts 'to carry their lives for the amusement of the readers'."

It feels like everything in football is heightened: time is spent highlighting perceived biases from media companies; time is wasted reading Garth Crooks and watching *Match of the Day* only to find more bias to get annoyed about; the narratives are being formed and we must point them out in real time; the officials are in a conspiracy against us, costing us vital points in the title race; ignoring grievous bodily harm on our players; and yet, despite all of this, nobody mentions the *actual* football. No mention of the pleasure taken watching *that* exquisite touch, that turn, that finish. No mention of the tactical battle between two managerial superbrains. No mention of the pinged cross-field pass that was like a magnet to the intended target. It all gets ignored, and forgotten, while we buy into the soap opera. While we get entertained. While we amuse ourselves to death ....

Or does it? Because – still – even in this technological screen-driven society, and living with local and national lockdowns, sport is not entertainment to me. Supporting Liverpool Football Club is not about being entertained, although, thankfully, since Klopp took over it overwhelmingly has been. I don't want to be entertained. The basic premise of sport is the unpredictable nature of it: the ability to win eighteen matches consecutively, twice, might suggest differently. To win 110 points from a possible 114 emphasises how predictable it got. And yet, that's more reason to focus on the football itself. Because it was such a remarkable sequence of results, never before seen in the history of the most decorated football club in the land. In the space of less than a decade we've had Roy Hodgson, and *that* defeat at home to Wolves, when barely anyone turned up. Such was the dire nature of the football, the club and the manager. We've had league cup wins and FA Cup final defeats under Sir Kenny Dalglish, and a season of black swan crossbar woe. We've had 'SSS' under Rodgers' tutelage, over a hundred league goals of majestic magnificence all culminating in *that* slip. We all slipped with Steven Gerrard. We all felt that pain. The only predictable thing before that defeat to Chelsea was that Liverpool would score a goal. Liverpool always scored in games that season, often four and five at a time. It was predictable. It was bound to happen. We would not let that slip. We did; he did. Figuratively and literally. All these moments of built up pain, unpredictable and agonising. No script. No writers. No narrative arc. Just an incredible desire to win the league.

Football is sport. Football will *always* be sport. We will of course be entertained by it at times, unless you support Crystal Palace. Surely nobody will ever be entertained by Hodgeball? And that's the point. We didn't just stop supporting Liverpool in those dark times. We endured it, rallied against it, and fought off the cowboys and face-stroker. Now we get to savour the monumental success under FSG and Klopp. But, I do ask myself the question: if we didn't have Klopp now, if we still had Hodgson, would I be as engaged with this new form of fan-free football? Screen-fan football through the medium of social media. I'd like to think so, because the club needs the support, even with the many millions running through its coffers. Football needs the support. Especially lower down the leagues.

One of the main curators of *The Social Dilemma,* Tristan Harris, was on *The Joe Rogan Experience* podcast recently, and highlighted that many of the issues raised in the documentary were covered in the book *Amusing Ourselves to Death* written by Neil Postman all the way back in 1985. He used the opening lines of the book to sum up and finish the podcast:

"What Orwell feared were those who would ban books. What Huxley feared was that there would be no reason to ban a book, for there would be no one who wanted to read one. Orwell feared those who would deprive us of information. Huxley feared those who would give us so much that we would be reduced to passivity and egoism. Orwell feared that the truth would be concealed from us. Huxley feared the truth would be drowned in a sea of irrelevance. Orwell feared we would become a captive culture. Huxley feared we would become a trivial culture."

Football is not trivial. Someone once might have said it is the 'most important of the least important things'. It can be amusing, and trivial, and we are often amused by the trivial parts but there's far more to it. Personally, it's that feeling in the pit of the stomach before a game. The anticipation and anxiety building while we think of all the possible scenarios that could play out. Debates about team selections and tactics. Watching in awe as we break at speed, precision throughballs, deft control, flicks and dribbles, before laser-like finishes cap off wondrous moves that we get to replay in our heads for eternity. They become so embedded that fans can reel off high definition descriptions of goals scored decades ago. That relaxed feeling of joy when we are four or five nil up, cruising towards the end of the game, three points wrapped up and we sit back, light the cigar, pour our favourite drink and discuss how amazing the game was with close friends.

It goes further though, because breaking the match down, looking at the stats, analysing the tactics, the substitutes, the performances, the best and worst moments, that's all part of the package now. It always has been for me, it's just now with TTT (and other sites) the sheer volume of participants and quality of opinions is far greater than it ever has been. When I was eighteen it was four or five mates, a newspaper and the odd radio or TV show. Now it has evolved into hundreds of online mates, with far more nuanced, evidence-based views and detailed resources to draw upon who help enhance the experience more; the newspaper is now non existent, and podcasts (selected over years of finding those worth the time) have replaced radio and TV shows for punditry. And of all the possible distractions from the real-life horrors on the news, of all the possible options available to get a release from the negative elements of our own lifes, then my pick is football, even without fans. Because remember, we are still on pause. We still have it all to come. That moment when we get to celebrate together. When we get a release that's been building for thirty years. One word of advice: don't film it. Savour it. Put the screen down. Get your bluenose mate to film it for you! I'd happily be amused to death by football. In fact, it's been killing me for thirty years and I wouldn't have it any other way. What a way to go...

Was 2020 The Best Title Win Ever?

By Chris Rowland

A draw would be enough. A draw it was: 1-1, until the 78th minute. Then, a penalty, and a sending off of the player who handled on the line. We all know what came next. Chelsea's Willian scored the penalty, Manchester City went 2-1 down with 12 minutes and 10 men left. They needed to score twice more. They didn't score once. And with that, our entrail-twisting wait was over, replaced by air-punching delirium. Thirty years of hurt evaporated into the summer night, destined for the waste bin of history.

This all happened on June 26th, 2020. A date when every season bar this exceptional one had long since been concluded. Over 100 football-less days had passed between our last league game, Bournemouth at Anfield on March 7th, and the first after lockdown, at Goodison on June 21st.

This yawning eternity was studded with fears about whether we would be robbed of what we so richly deserved from our first 29 games – won 27, drawn one, lost one, and the loss only coming in game 28 – not by football results but a global pandemic and the naked self-interest or equally unclothed Liverpool-hating null-and-voiders. We heard other European leagues who'd decided to cancel the season and have no champions or relegation. The spectre of the same happening to us lurked in every dark demonic corner for week after week after locked-down week. Unknown and uncharted territory stretched out before us for nobody knew how long.

In the end it was decided the season would be concluded. When the moment finally came, the deferred explosion of joy came amidst the surreal setting of midsummer and empty stadia. In my life, in my house, for the first and so far only time in my life I had ordered some pyro, online. A red smoke grenade arrived the day of the Chelsea-City match. Queen's 'We Are The Champions' was duly set up on the turntable. Problem was, being a pyro virgin, it took me so long to shift the bloody ring-pull that the next track was on by the time the red smoke began spewing forth from a hanging basket, at a 45-degree angle due to the strong wind, and accompanied now by 'Sheer Heart Attack'! – perhaps even more appropriate in the circumstances!

We'd done our bit, beating Palace 4-0 at Anfield the night before, and still had seven more games left for us to get over the line, with a 20+ point lead. Number 19 duly arrived the following night, in the oddest circumstances in the game's entire history. As it turned out, we had already amassed enough points *before* lockdown to win it, as City finished with 81 points, 18 behind the Reds.

So where does 2020 sit in the great scheme of things, against all those other title wins, for a match-going supporter (not that any of us has been that since March 2020, and it doesn't feel like that will be changing any time soon)? I thought back to the near misses. Rafa Benítez's Fernando Torres/Steven Gerrard team that got so close in 2009, Brendan Rodgers' Luis Suarez/Daniel Sturridge version that got even closer in 2014 before *that* moment, all those jibes of 'you've never won the Premier League' (bad enough from fans from Manchester and London, but hard to take from fans of Blackburn and Leicester).

I also thought back to the last time, in 1990. A lacklustre home game against lacklustre opposition rounded off a fairly lacklustre season, and in truth an unexceptional team – if lacklustre occasions and unexceptional teams can be seen as compatible with the idea of being champions. At the time, it kind of was. Our 11th title in 17 seasons was as near to a non-event as winning a title could be. There were much better seasons and titles won by much better Liverpool teams than the 1990 incarnation. A 2-1 win against QPR sealed the title with two games still remaining. The players, many of them ageing stars on the cusp of melting or in some cases closer to liquid, ran around with the trophy after the match, taking half-hearted applause from a half-empty Anfield. Yes, yes, we've seen all this many times before thanks, and better than this. Blasé, complacent? Yeah, we probably were.

But there was no reason for anyone, inside Anfield or elsewhere in the English game, to think No.19 wouldn't happen again before long.

The winners of Liverpool's previous title, two years earlier, were diametrically opposed to the 1990 version, so far ahead of the rest that the league had long since ceased being a competitive event by the time it was done. There had been no doubt about the outcome at any stage during the season. Kenny Dalglish's team of thoroughbreds, of John Barnes and Peter Beardsley, cantered through to the finish line slowing up, without the slightest need for an anxious glance back over the shoulder. They played some wonderful football, that Anfield 5-0 rout of a decent Nottingham Forest remaining a joyous high point of creative free-flowing football.

But you need competition to create excitement. Just standing back and purring in admiration doesn't stir the adrenaline. This was more of a parade than a contest, awesome in its scale and spectacle and with no sign of opposition!

I was too young to really experience the successes of the mid-60s. My first title as a Kop-going teenager came with Bill Shankly's first trophy with his new team, in 1972/73. Kevin Keegan and John Toshack, Steve Heighway and Emlyn Hughes, Ray Clemence and Peter Cormack, Larry Lloyd and Alec Lindsay. A 2-0 win against Leeds at Anfield in front of nearly 56,000 all but clinched it, with a home game against Leicester still to come in case the goal average calculators were really needed. They weren't.

The next title win, in 1976, was Bob Paisley's first of six titles in nine seasons. It reached a searing climax in the last game, at Molineux, when the title was only sealed in the last 15 minutes. It was a truly unforgettable night as countless thousands of Reds, including yours truly with his left arm in plaster, filled the South Bank and, when we scored those three goals before that massed end and deprived QPR of the title, the pitch.

Winning the title away always seemed more enjoyable as a supporter, and I was behind the goal into which Kenny Dalglish volleyed the title clincher at Stamford Bridge in May 1986. The fact that we had won it back from Everton and pipped them by two points, by winning nine of the previous 11 games to reel them in, certainly added a dimension. And for good measure we went on to beat them in the first Merseyside FA Cup Final soon after.

Other titles were confirmed in low-key games, which generally result in low-key climaxes: in 1976/77, a goalless draw at Coventry all but sealed it, and another goalless draw at Anfield against West Ham in the next match did. It was as it sounds, at least when compared to what was happening all around it – an FA Cup semi-final against Everton, which went to a replay, that iconic European Cup quarter-final against St Etienne, then a season-ending FA Cup final against Man United followed by our first European Cup final, and win, against Moenchengladbach in Rome. The league kind of got lost in the maelstrom.

In 1978/79 and '79/80, by weird coincidence two resounding Anfield wins against Aston Villa with two games left sealed both titles, the first 3-0, the second 4-1. 1978/79 was the season of the 7-0 home win against Spurs and *that* Terry McDermott goal, but also saw first round elimination from the European Cup we had won for the last two seasons, by Brian Clough's Nottingham Forest, who went on to win it at their first attempt, then retain it the following year. Quite galling, since we'd worked our roes out for over a decade to finally scale that mountain! 1979/80 had the added sweetness of keeping runners-up United's run of title-less years going.

The 1982 title win was probably the best comeback of them all. On Boxing Day, after losing 3-1 at home to Man City, Liverpool had dropped to 12th in the table (for context, in the previous nine seasons, we'd finished 1st five times and 2nd three times, although the season before had only finished 5th, although also winning the European Cup and League Cup). But the recovery in the second half of the season was such that by beating Spurs 3-1 at Anfield in the penultimate game, we clinched a 7th title in a decade.

Liverpool made it three successive titles in '82/83 and in '83/84. 1982/83 featured the 5-0 win at Goodison – *Rush scored one, Rush scored two, Rush scored three and Rush scored four!* – but the title clincher was a defeat, 2-0 at Spurs, when United could only draw at Norwich. There were three games left. In the end Watford were distant runners up, 11 points behind. As in 2020, Liverpool tailed off once the deal was done, losing two and drawing the other of the last three games.

In 1984, Joe Fagan won a treble in his first season, with the European Cup in Rome and a League Cup as well as yet another title, but again one which was won in distinctly underwhelming fashion, with a goalless draw at relegated Notts County in the penultimate fixture.

There were some great Liverpool teams in there, with great players playing some great football. The late '70s team of Dalglish and David Johnson, Ray Kennedy, Jimmy Case, McDermott, Phil Neal, Phil Thompson, Emlyn Hughes and Ray Clemence. The early-'80s pomp of Graeme Souness, Dalglish, Ian Rush, Alan Hansen and Mark Lawrenson. But it was the journey that trumped the destination in almost every case, Molineux in 1976 excepted. The league was often referred to by both Paisley and his predecessor Bill Shankly as the club's "bread and butter". It was usually Europe that delivered the filling.

If the question is, was 2020's the best Liverpool title-winning side ever, well you'd have to say, despite fierce competition – from Dalglish's 1987/88 Barnes and Beardsley vintage's eye-candy football, but without the demands of a European campaign, and from those imperious late '70s and early '80s teams, which most certainly did have Europe to contend with – the stats alone suggest it was.

No illustrious forerunners quite managed what the 2019/20 team did. After reaching 82 points after 29 pre-lockdown games – a staggering points-per-game (PPG) of 2.83! (though it dropped to 17 from the last nine games, or a PPG of just 1.89) – the final total of 99 points, a PPG of 2.61, comfortably exceeds any previous Liverpool team apart from the previous season's 97, but that was more or less the same team anyway!

But if you asked me what was my most exciting, thrilling dénouement to a title-winning season as a fan, my vote goes to

Molineux in 1976. However, no other title win brought the satisfaction, relief and sense of merit that 2020 – not least because we never had to wait 30 years for any of the others! Its unprecedented absence of crowds and victory parade did detract from it, and I felt particularly sorry for those younger fans who have never witnessed this moment, who've heard their dads drone on and on about Molineux '76 and Stamford Bridge '86 and now were deprived of being there to see it for themselves.

My Favourite Title Win

By TTT subscriber Allen Baynes

Maybe the first time …

They say you always remember the first time, whether it's love, your first pay packet, your first car, your first house etc. Usually, in all of these things, it gets better and the first does not always remain the best. I am incredibly lucky, and I have bored this site on many occasions about my memories of iconic games that I was fortunate to be at. So undoubtedly for me, watching Liverpool Football Club has got better and better in the course of my life; in fact, except for Roy Hodgson's calamitous era, I have always felt we would continue to improve and happily we mostly have.

However, in terms of league title wins the 18th April 1964 will, for me, remain the best. I was 13, a Kirkby urchin, very near the start of my life's journey. In those days with no social media, non-existent TV coverage and *The Liverpool Echo* the only newspaper in our house, the best way, as always, to follow the Reds was to go to the game. I started going to the game religiously in the 1963/64 season. Lucky? Too right. This was the season when Bill Shankly came to the fore. His revolution was in full swing and the bastion that was Anfield was well under construction.

Up until this season, I had only been to games with my Dad; now it was time to go with my mates from Kirkby. You can imagine the big boy bravado that we had, we knew that the world was changing, and we were part of it. We had the Beatles, Jimmy Tarbuck – and like us they came from Liverpool. The city was still emerging from the war, there were reminders everywhere from the bombies, (bomb sites) that seemed to litter every corner where I grew up in Litherland and Walton, never more than a mile from the docks. Times were undoubtedly hard but as it seemed to be the same for everyone, we just accepted it as the norm.

We didn't have much spare money but we had a leader: Bill Shankly. He made you feel that you were special, part of the team behind the team, the 12th man, even if your voice hadn't broken and you were only in the Boys' Pen. You were part of a new culture, the singing, swaying football crowd. It was unbelievably special and we instinctively knew it. We didn't need the latest mobile phone, or the latest gear or the best trainers. Mobiles didn't exist, we had no money for the latest gear and trainers were baseball boots at best, pumps if you didn't have them. It was the time to be a Scouser, the best time in my life moving from childhood to manhood and we were part of the best induction process to manhood that I could ever imagine as part of the Kop.

The season itself (the last before *Match of the Day* began at the start of 1964/65 with Liverpool vs Arsenal) is shrouded by the fog of time; no newsreel or television pictures to jog your memory, only football annuals and match programmes to stir the memory of what seems a very different time. I remember losing to Swansea in the 6th round of the cup – Peter Thompson scoring but also hitting the post and it rebounding along the line to safety; Ronnie Moran putting a penalty high into the Kop and their keeper, Noel Dwyer, (I think), having a worldie. I also remember one of the best goals that I have ever seen at Anfield, in a 5-0 defeat of Derby County in January 1964. It was right at the end of the game and we were at the bottom of the pen ready for a quick dart down the valley for the bus (Everton Valley). A long ball came from defence towards the Kop and Alfie Arrowsmith was in full flight, and as the ball dropped, either by design or by fluke, he caught it with his heel in full stride and the ball arced over his head and that of the keeper. It was a goal worthy of Pele, but it was only Alfie and with no TV coverage, there's probably only he and I who remember it.

The match-day experience was a far cry from today's customer-focused experience. It started on the 92 or 15D bus from Kirkby, with your mates all excited about the event of the week, the match. As now, we either walked up the Valley or along Walton Breck Road, no towering stand, no club shop, just the old, terraced streets and pubs that we were yet to gain entry to. And so, it was to the chippy, Costa's, opposite the Kop – a bag of chips swimming in vinegar and costing all of 4d and then a shilling into the pen (4d = 2p and one shilling = 5p in 2020). We were in the ground usually about 1.30pm, a good hour and a half before the kick-off, but at least the steps were still dry then! To be fair they never got too wet as, unlike the Kopites, we hadn't had 10 pints before the game! The delights of the wet echo and wet jeans on the back of your legs were to be part of our initiation into the Kop in the 1965/66 season.

The big day, 18th April 1964: the day we won the league for the first time in my life. It was another match day with the same ritual of bus, chippy, pen, win. Only this win was special, it was the seventh win on the bounce. It was April and still three games to go, but all we had to do was beat the Arsenal. As you can imagine, or indeed recall if you have seen the *Panorama* documentary of the day, the ground was bouncing. The Kop in full voice, as were we, swaying to all the latest hits, many made by Liverpool groups, we knew all the words. These would start about 2.30pm, other songs were played before, but this was the Kop playlist, *She Loves You*, *Twist and Shout*, Ken Dodd's *Happiness* and of course Gerry with what was to become our famous anthem.

Before the game, some lad or young man climbed up the girders holding up the roof of the Kop and there he sat to watch the game. I thought he actually sat on the roof, but I can find no evidence except in the deep recesses of my mind. The atmosphere was electric but not as good as our European nights or as organised as the more choreographed match-day build ups today. Of course, then, only the Kop sang, today it is the whole ground but back then it was an incredibly special fan-led experience. It was part of my life, it started a lifelong love affair with Liverpool FC; I couldn't know that 56 years later I would still be going to the match, (in spirit only this season), singing *You'll Never Walk Alone* before the game and loving every minute of it.

The game? Well we battered Arsenal, we scored five – should have had 10! It was just as in the words of the song, "Hunt, St John and Thompson score the goals when Shankly wants them", of course Alfie got one but his name didn't scan in the same way as the others, so he is a largely forgotten man, though not by me.

So, it may not feature as everybody's best league win, but it was mine because it led to Wembley, Istanbul, Qatar and lots of places from Paris down to Turkey and more Silver than in Peñasquito.

High Farce, Drama and Surrealism: 2020/21
By Paul Tomkins

Jürgen Klopp's Liverpool, statistically the best team England has ever seen (110 league points from 114 in a rolling 38-game period, that included nine games before being crowned European champions, and 29 *as reigning European champions*, all of which saw them rise to 4th in the all-time European ELO index rankings), appeared to be having their title defence destroyed by injuries, lack of preparation time, Covid-19 quarantines and some absolutely batshit-insane refereeing and VAR decisions. The start, it has to be said, did not go smoothly.

The early schedule also threw up a sequence so bizarre that by the time the Reds faced Everton in the fifth game, every single opponent – whether a Big Six team, derby rival or an unfancied side that just escaped relegation – had won every single one of their matches (although Leeds, on day one, obviously hadn't played anyone yet). Arsenal, arriving at Anfield with a 100% record, were beaten 3-1, and Chelsea, with a 100% record, were toyed with and dispatched 2-0 at Stamford Bridge, and then came … well, Aston Villa, with their 100% record (followed by a two-week break and a trip to Everton with their 100% record).

I wrote last season about the halloween timing of Liverpool's *Thriller*-themed dead-and-buried comeback at Aston Villa from

1-0 down with just a couple of minutes to play to win 2-1, but this was on a whole other scale of surreality and frankly, damn-right terror. This was a literal horror show, albeit the scoreline was not reflective of the game in any sense at all. Liverpool admittedly started badly, with Alisson's stand-in, Adrián, gifting Villa an early goal, and then the ref, Martin Atkinson (himself a walking horror show, who had given Roberto Firmino's armpit as offside in the same fixture a year earlier, as the VAR) ignored a clear scything down of Mo Salah in the box, and the VAR on this occasion apparently okayed it within seconds, as if to prove that he and the assistant VAR at Stockley Park *could not* have watched many angles. (On *Sky* commentary, Jamie Carragher, who seems to often suggest that Salah goes down too easily – which I'd disagree with, as too often he stays on his feet when fouled – said there was nothing in it; then, with every replay he admitted he was wrong and it was a clear penalty.)

Villa were soon able to score again, and so a 76% chance of it being 1-1 from the spot (or 95% chance with Mo Salah on penalty duties) was lost, and it was suddenly 2-0 to the home side – a real wind-stealing sucker punch.

Despite my best efforts to focus less on officiating this season, 2020/21 was proving to be a nadir for common sense and, indeed, 20-20 vision. At least Liverpool did not suffer any of the handball nonsense before that rule was relaxed after the outcry (although did somehow still suffer it later in the season) – and actually, in the opening game against Leeds, Jürgen Klopp's men got their first league handball penalty in years (and first at Anfield since May 2017); albeit a clear one, where a raised arm clearly blocked a goal-bound shot. But also swiftly out the window seemed to go the referees viewing the pitch-side monitors, which was long overdue, and a clear improvement, and which would have helped the Reds at Goodison Park – only for that to return, to Liverpool's detriment, weeks later. Consistency and logic had gone out the window.

On a couple of occasions Liverpool fought their way back into the game at Villa, placing mounting pressure on the hosts, resulting in a goal, only for a hugely deflected shot – that sent the ball in the opposite direction to the keeper, and each time tucked *just inside* the post – to put the hosts back in total control and kill the Reds' resistance. Indeed, Villa had time for another deflected goal later in the game, that matched the first two in turning a saveable shot into an unsaveable goal. On expected goals (xG) the game ended roughly 2.5 to Liverpool and 3.5 to Villa (so on balance, a one-goal victory for Dean Smith's team would have been fair), but of course, luck can play a big part in finishing. Liverpool also did not get that "0.76 of a goal" that is a clear unchallenged shot from 12 yards with the keeper forced to stay on his line, and which, at 1-0, could have changed the game.

But the score ended 7-2 to the Villans (just weeks after Liverpool won a game, in the League Cup, 7-2, having also won a preseason friendly 7-2, which has to be utterly unique), and it made no sense on the balance of play; although at 5-2, having suffered *another* deflected goal, Liverpool – so rarely seen under Jürgen Klopp – looked mentally beaten, and by that stage were indeed all over the place. (Mentality minnows, for once, instead of mentality monsters.) With the *scoreline* more than Villa killing them, it was as if there was nothing they could physically do to alter the bad officiating from Atkinson, nor the black swan event of three heavily deflected goals (although perhaps each could have been closed down better, but weirdly, the shots would have been less harmful had they not been closed down at all). It felt like even if Villa aimed at the corner flag it would somehow deflect in.

And in fairness to Villa, in the final minutes they tore past Liverpool's increasingly high and erratic defensive line, to the point where the Reds' heads had gone so much they were playing offside *in the opposition half.* Villa, whilst clearly super-lucky with three of the goals, were largely excellent, and clearly found a way to get in behind the high-stakes high line the Reds had been deploying for some time (mostly to great effect, but less so since wrapping up the title – which was partly natural, in terms of a drop in intensity); but to put a huge of chunk of the scoreline in perspective, it would be a miracle of luck if Liverpool were to score three such heavily – and *decisively* – deflected goals in the entire remainder of the season. With 33 in the goals-against column when winning the title, Liverpool didn't concede a single deflected shot in the whole of 2019/20; and of the 85 scored on the way to becoming champions, Curtis Jones' strike (ironically against Villa) was the only one deflected – meaning just a single deflected goal in the 118 scored at both ends during the Reds' 38 games. That was already *trebled* within just four games in 2020/21.

Villa had found that jet-black swan, to score three such goals in just 31 minutes of football, and Liverpool must have run over a black cat.

There were also a few sloppy moments from Virgil van Dijk, and little did we know that his entire career would be in the balance two weeks later. Part of the problem had to be the three games for Holland that were ludicrously crammed in between the Villa nightmare and an entirely different form of nightmare for the Reds' totemic defensive leader (even impact injuries can be worsened if the player has had a heavy workload). Facing anywhere between nine and 18 months out, van Dijk's peak years – his imperial phase – have been robbed, by a lunatic who poses as an Everton goalkeeper, with a reputation for flying out of his goal with reckless abandon. Van Dijk may never again reach the levels of being the world's best, given that he could be 31 by the time he's back, and the body, and knee in particular, may never be the same (there is a small but very real chance that players never fully recover from such injuries); but you know he'll damned-well try. And we'd all love to see it, just so that, in 2022, Trent Alexander-Arnold can swing in a beautiful cross for van Dijk to – legally – head both the ball *and* Jordan Pickford into the net.

The anterior cruciate ligament, along with the posterior cruciate ligament, are basically what holds the lower leg together; without them, this classic "leg-breaker" of a challenge was actually worse than a leg-breaker, in that a certain type of broken leg can heal within just a few months. The fact that Pickford was allowed to get away with it presumably emboldened Richarlison to try something similar on Thiago, although thankfully Michael Oliver saw *this* one, clear and up close; but the Spanish-Brazilian maestro was also sidelined for more than a handful of games as a result of having studs smash into his knee, having only just recovered from Covid-19.

Oliver, who had earlier in the season done the thing that only he usually does – *give Liverpool Anfield penalties* (and Kop-end, too) – somehow missed Jordan Pickford's reckless endangerment, and the incident was also more inexplicably missed via David Coote, the VAR, who was presumably too busy trying to find an offside from a situation that appeared dead-level so as to not give Liverpool a penalty – which he duly achieved; even though he and his assistant had access to multiple angles, unlike Oliver. There was confusion and contradicting messages, as usual, from the Premier League, as they tried to get their story straight. It was later declared that the incident *was* seen and reviewed, even though any sane observer would have said it warranted a red card, had that been the case. And as it was deemed to be seen, Pickford escaped a three-game retrospective ban. Bonkers.

Interestingly, having gone a couple of years without any opponent being sent off against the Reds, two came along in the first five games: Chelsea's Andreas Christensen given a straight red for a last-man foul on Sadio Mané, and Richarlison obviously given his marching orders in the derby. Interestingly, the clearest red card – particularly on replays – was Pickford's, but *on the pitch* at least, only one of these three red cards was shown: Oliver missed the Pickford one, but as well as sending off Richarlison, he did at least step in as the VAR to overturn Paul Tierney's yellow card for Christensen; you could generously suggest Tierney was miles behind the play – and he was – because Jordan Henderson played a long incisive pass that pretty much only Mané could keep up with, and the angle he had was clearly not the best to see the rugby tackle on the Liverpool striker, nor to see if the keeper, Kepa, would have made it to the ball first (he would not have). Tierney was called to view the pitchside monitor by Oliver, and it's a shame that Oliver wasn't asked to do the same by Coote at Goodison Park.

Coote was the same VAR who had failed to see a foul on Divock Origi at Old Trafford last season that allowed Manchester United to score; and, as ref, failed to see Andy Robertson get literally booted up in the air in the Kop-end box against Burnley, which ended Liverpool's 22-game winning run at Anfield, and led the Liverpool left-back to question what the point was in Coote even being on the pitch (as the cameras and microphones trailed the two men walking off at the end of the game. It would be unthinkable that Coote could bear a grudge, *obviously*).

Indeed, in his short career, all Coote has done is pretty much rule out legitimate Liverpool goals, allow the opposition to score goals that involved fouls, and fail to send off a goalkeeper for a two-footed knee-high 'scissors' assault on the world's best defender. This may just be an unfortunate sequence of mishaps rather than bias or some agenda, but it doesn't look good.

Coote's *coup de grâce* at Goodison was still to come. The derby was heading towards a 2-2 draw – thanks to several Pickford saves, which seemed inevitable once he escaped the red card – when Richarlison was dismissed, late on; Oliver getting that one spot-on. And with the extra man, the Reds scored a legitimate last-gasp winner, when Pickford badly fumbled Jordan Henderson's shot into the net – not just a glorious winner but poetic justice, too. Sadio Mané was clearly level with three Everton defenders when he received the ball, but after minutes of line drawing and redrawing, the bizarre conclusion was "offside".

Liverpool subsequently asked the Premier League and PGMOL what part of Mané's body was offside; it could only possibly be the tip of his elbow, if *anything*, and even with what constitutes handball now lowered from the shoulder to the t-shirt line on the biceps, you cannot be offside with your elbow. It all felt too shoddy, and ex-referee and refs' head honcho Keith Hackett led the calls in *The Daily Telegraph* about how it was becoming a farce:

"The challenge by Jordan Pickford on Virgil van Dijk was clearly an act of serious foul play for which a straight red card was the appropriate sanction.

"… On field the two assistants and fourth official could have intervened and at Stockley Park video assistant referee David Coote and his assistant really should have dealt with the referee's serious and obvious error.

"The offside decision against Sadio Mané in the build-up to Jordan Henderson's disallowed goal was another incorrect call.

"…I do not believe that the system that operates well and the lines drawn on screen produce the accuracy that is required, because goal-line technology cameras operate at 500 frames per second while offside cameras are operating at 50 frames per second. We should adopt the system which is in other countries and bin the lines that are drawn on the screen until technology catches up.

"… My view is that Mané is level with the Everton defenders and therefore not offside."

Presumably due to the Pickford incident and not the phantom offsides, Coote would be relieved of his duties for the following weekend and demoted to the Championship the week after, but this brought back neither the precious two points he cost Liverpool, nor the bragging rights to the red half of the city (and the red portion of the globe). As there was literally no time for Everton to equalise after Henderson's "goal" it was an undeniable match-winner that was stolen away. It felt like being gaslit.

As I noted on TTT, watching football with VAR right now is like watching a vandal take a knife to a Rembrandt. Not only is it vandalism, maybe it is also its own kind of art: Dadaism, perhaps, where the creators eschew logic and reason in favour of irrationality and nonsense. (One presumes Mike Riley could adequately be replaced by a ceramic urinal placed in a gallery.) When asked to explain their decisions, Martin Atkinson will say "parsnips", and David Coote will add that, "the grey smoke seeps silently and wistfully from an exhaust pipe, like a dawn mist on the moorlands".

A week later, Liverpool were 1-0 down thanks again to VAR. It felt like reality was being warped by someone in Stockley Park,

200 miles away. Klopp's men came from behind against Sheffield United to win for the second home game in a row, having earlier conceded the lead to Arsenal, and Liverpool did not rue the return of Rhian Brewster, the ex-Red rooster. It was something of a shock to see him sold after the progress he made during his loan at Swansea, albeit for a healthy £23m, but the club insists, as policy, on a buyback clause for all its talented youngsters; in this case, about £10m more than Sheffield United paid. That means that for around £35m, Liverpool could buy back the 22- or- 23-year-old Brewster if he has established himself at the top level, having looked elite at Championship level. The Blades get to "keep" the player in the meantime, but unlike a two-year loan, which can also be used to develop players, in this instance there is a greater incentive for the Yorkshire club to get the best out of the striker, as he's *technically* theirs. By contrast, if he were to excel on a two-year loan, they would lose him for nothing (instead of c. £35m) if he went back to Liverpool to replace one of the famed front three, all of whom will be 30 in 2022. And of course, with the coronavirus kicking clubs in the wallet, Liverpool were open to an influx of cash to meet the costs of a huge wage bill (which is only actually huge because it's heavily incentivised, and the *crazy, crazy* players keep winning the biggest trophies and earning those huge bonuses, the damn fools. One big issue after 2019/20 was that a fair chunk of the club's own promised bonuses from the Premier League – the prize money from the TV deal – had to be paid back, even though more games were being televised).

In an interview with *The Athletic*, Brewster explained his decision, but also highlighted the special situation he had left behind:

"I will take a lot of things [from being at Liverpool], even games, like the Barcelona game when I was on the bench," he said. "The whole experience. Training against them, playing against Virg [Virgil van Dijk], seeing Sadio [Mané], Bobby [Roberto Firmino] and Mo [Salah] in training. There is not one person who slacks off in training or even in the gym.

"Say, for example, James Milner. He is in his 30s and still going strong and that's for a reason. Because he is always in the gym, always doing what he has to do, always eating right, doing everything he can to be the best."

The surrealism of the season continued upon Brewster's return to Anfield, just days after Liverpool had won 1-0 in Amsterdam against Ajax. Indeed, it spread to Holland: the Dutch giants promptly won their next game, away in the Eredivisie, 13 (THIRTEEN) - 0. The decision by the VAR, to turn Mike Dean's award of a free-kick half a yard outside the box into a penalty, felt utterly bonkers. Fabinho won the ball, and the replay clearly showed that it was outside the box. A tweet from Liverpool's TV presenter Matt Critchley said: "Clarification from the Premier League re: Sheff Utd penalty that was awarded. VAR only ruled on whether the incident was inside or outside the box, not on whether a foul took place or not."

The ball was clearly won by Fabinho – otherwise excelling as a stand-in centre-back – without touching the man; on first viewing it looked a foul, but well outside the box. On second viewing he clearly won the ball, and while it was a clumsy-looking challenge, it did not look like a foul from any of the other angles. Crucially, he did not appear to catch the opponent first. To make matters worse, Fabinho contacted the ball a good 8-12 inches *outside* the box, but the back of his foot was perhaps brushing the penalty box line, so it was given as a penalty. Which seemed utterly against the spirit of the game.

Just three days later it was back to the Champions League, as the big games were arriving almost every 72 hours. With a 2-0 victory over Danish side FC Midtjylland, the Reds topped the group after two games, with two wins, three goals scored, none conceded; but to add to the defensive crisis, Fabinho joined the injury list, in what was essentially The Group of Thomas Grønnemark (who coaches throw-ins with eight different clubs across Europe, three of whom just happen to be in Group D). On came teenager Rhys Williams, for over 60 minutes of action, following his last-minute debut in the competition in Holland a week earlier. A year earlier he was out on loan in the 6th tier of English football, to toughen up, as a raw 18-year-old. Mo Salah sealed the victory in the last minute with a run in on goal that saw his achilles raked by the despairing defender he was leaving in his wake, with just the keeper to beat; a clear penalty, yet many in the media (the pundits on *BT Sport*, and Chris Sutton on the BBC) suggested, as they bizarrely always do with Salah, that he went down too easily; never mind that he had no reason, with an easier chance to score – and that he hobbled off with a sore achilles. Rather than coronavirus, was everyone catching some kind of eye-related illness that inverts reality? (The same thing happened days later, where the West Ham defender admitted kicking Salah, and yet Salah was still castigated for going down.)

It was a win, but the Reds were down to the bare bones at centre-back. Reports suggested an increase of almost 50% in muscle injuries across the top division in the first six weeks of the 2020/21 season, as games were shoehorned into a frantic schedule after little or no preseason. West Ham's David Moyes admitted to voting that the Premier League allow just three substitutions, whilst the rest of Europe continued to allow five due to Covid-19 and less time between games. (As ever, West Ham doing everyone else a favour….)

Back on the pitch, Diogo Jota made an immediate impact with four vital goals in his first few games (all at the empty Kop end) – to kill the match against Arsenal, to win the game against Sheffield United and to effectively win the game against Midtjylland (although Mo Salah added a last-minute penalty to make it 2-0), then, having had a late goal disallowed against West Ham with the scores at 1-1, popped up again to net an ever later, *legitimate* winner – with five minutes to go, as if he'd been playing for Klopp's Liverpool for years.

And after the wilderness, injury-ravaged season of 2019/20, Xherdan Shaqiri opted to stay despite being free to leave; and so Harvey Elliott was loaned to Blackburn, for vital experience at the age of just 17, and Shaqiri found himself starting Champions League games, with the physical power and the old-pro nous that Elliott, as a young kid, naturally lacks. Suddenly, from being surplus to requirements, the Swiss was a handy option to have, as injuries to others came thick and fast. Now 29, Shaqiri is an ideal squad player, not least as *he* opted to stay – and that's always better than those who are forced to stay, and mope (although Klopp would rather get rid of anyone like that). He laid on a beautiful pass in the build-up to Jota's goal against Midtjylland, and then an even more sublime slide-rule nutmeg through-ball (quite literally, then, a *through*-ball) that set up the Portuguese's winner against West Ham.

One welcome statistic from Jota's bright start was that goal against Midtjylland was the Reds' 10,000th in all competitions (at an average of 72 per season since 1892, or just under two per game). Mané was already up to four goals in seven league games, and with the aid of three penalties, Salah was on seven. Indeed, when including Salah's thumped spot-kicks, he had rifled in *all* his goals with real venom and accuracy, which was in some contrast to his more usual left-foot curlers that he puts past the keeper with precision rather than pace (but also, often under-hits straight to the keeper at times, when it goes wrong). That power was needed again when the Reds won a penalty just before half-time against West Ham, and the Egyptian levelled the scores after yet another weirdly conceded goal: Pablo Fornals' mis-hit shot bobbling in off the post, to somehow become inch-perfect in its ineptitude by just eluding Alisson's grasp. Still, at least Liverpool already had three Anfield penalties, which is more than in some entire recent seasons.

Jota, by contrast to Salah's 2020/21 finishes, was adept at appearing in the six-yard box like a centre-forward who moves to the back post to steer the ball into the net; albeit unlike a normal poacher he was arriving from a wide starting point. He did this yet again to give Liverpool the lead against West Ham, with just 15 minutes to go, but *yet again* VAR ruled against the Reds; this time for a foul by Mané in a three-way challenge with Łukasz Fabiański and Angelo Ogbonna. And in fairness it probably *was* a foul, perhaps on both players, but after the weirdness of VAR denying Liverpool in the previous month it felt like some restitution was due – but these things never even themselves out, as there is no one to make that overarching judgement.

The season – so turbulent – had felt like a bit of a train wreck at times (ten goals conceded against just two teams who almost swapped places in the Premier League, had one not just escaped relegation), several slow starts, a raft of injuries and illness, and it was soul-sapping to see Anfield empty every time Jota popped in a vital goal. Blur's *Song 2* still blared, but it was starting to sound hollow after several months, and even worse when it was followed by the goal being disallowed three minutes later. (Still, what else can be done?) Yet the win against the Hammers left the Reds three points clear on the night, two points clear after the weekend, and one point clear after match-week seven's games were finalised on the Monday, whilst also topping the Champions League group after two games. Big matches against Atalanta and Manchester City loomed before the international break.

And incredibly, the win against West Ham meant the Reds had equalled their all-time record of 63 league home games unbeaten, matching a run from 1978 to 1981; and in addition, the last ten times the Reds had been behind at home they had come back to win. Before long, this team could own *all* the club's all-time records, as well as several of the country's.

This was added to the club's two highest ever league points tallies, that also ranked third and fourth overall; the most goals any club had scored in a Champions League/European Cup season; the fewest games required to win the English title (i.e. the *quickest*); the biggest 38-game rolling total by any English club (110, up from the previous record of 102); the most league points by any English team in a season (97) in which the big European trophy was also won, with 90 the previous best; and the club's most consecutive league home wins (22). And then there was the rank of 4th-best of all time in the Elo rankings, plus the most spectacular European semi-final comeback ever seen. (Doubtless there are further records that I have overlooked.)

Going into the final week before the latest international break (which seemed insane in the circumstances), Liverpool had found form, if not fluency. The Reds travelled to free-scoring Atalanta, the Italian team with the most modern playing style. Those Italians were duly demolished 5-0, albeit the xG was a bit similar (albeit reversed) to the Aston Villa defeat, in that it was roughly 2.5 to 1.0, suggesting a 2-1 or 3-1 victory would have been just. Alisson made a couple of big saves, and the one shot that did beat him rebounded strangely back from the underside of the bar, across the goalline, to go harmlessly out of play. At the other end, the Reds were largely ruthless, although only scored five of their six big chances (six being more than Klopp's Liverpool had accrued in all previous visits to Italy combined, with a trip to Roma and two trips to Napoli). Both Salah and Mané scored expertly-taken goals (Salah's curled in, after breaking from his own half from an Atalanta corner), but Jota stole the show with a sensational hat-trick – his third in eight European games, after two with Wolves last season.

When watching Jota the other week – so even before the hat-trick in the 5-0 away thumping of fancied Italians Atalanta – the player who sprang to mind was Fernando Torres, a fellow Iberian who also arrived at Liverpool aged 23, and exploded onto the scene. While Jota is a couple of inches shorter, there's something of the pace and directness, and a physical sturdiness that they maybe didn't have as teenage prodigies. Torres arrived with more fanfare, as a big hero in Madrid, but their careers have some surprising similarities. Torres was the right age, and it was the right time.

I'm always fascinated by the quietly bubbling-under goalscorer: the player who has incredible stats for his age, in international youth football or maybe at an unfashionable club, or possibly even in the second tier, but then has to take his game to the next level. The all-round game has to be worked on, and sometimes the goals dry up, especially in a struggling side (even more so if promoted to the top flight, as both Torres and Jota were early in their careers), unless they are taking penalties and/or are the total focus of the attack. Even then, despite a few doing so in the 1990s, it's now rare for anyone aged 17-19 to bag tons of goals. Jota is one of those early bloomers who just needed a bit of time to mature into a truly special player.

Remember, just a couple of months ago people were laughing that Liverpool signed the wrong Wolves attacker; now, with seven goals from less than a handful of starts, it seems that – who knew it? – the Liverpool recruitment department understand what they are doing. Adama Traoré, the player some felt should have been signed, is bigger, stronger and faster, but Jota, a year younger, has already got more goals in just a season-and-a-bit (23) than Traoré has *in his entire professional career* (22). Traoré is eye-catching, and improving, but Jota scores goals and presses like a demon.

Jota, like Torres at Atlético Madrid, spent a lot of time at a team fighting to finish 6th, and trudging through Europe's lesser competition; and in Wolves' case, they weren't a domineering force, but upstarts. Even so, Jota bagged two hat-tricks in last season's Europa League, which suggested that when Wolves were more evenly matched with their opponents, he could really make a difference.

Between U16 and U19 levels, Torres scored 19 goals in 19 games for Spain, but he scored just one in his first 14 full caps. As a kid, Torres scored just six in his first full season in the second tier (36 games), but even though he became a legend and a talisman for Atléti, he never scored more than 13 non-penalty league goals in a season before signing for Liverpool, aged 23. Suddenly, without taking penalties, he was straight in with 24 Premier League goals, and 33 overall. With better players around him, and in a team aiming higher than 6th, he caught fire. He suddenly scored at a rate not seen since he was in the Spanish youth sides.

Jota also played for Atlético Madrid – or at least, he was with them for two years, both spent out on loan, before he joined Wolves on a permanent basis. Jota was also prolific at U19 and U21 level, with an impressive 13 in 29 games, presumably not as a centre-forward. (Traoré, by contrast, managed just one goal in 19 age-group games for Spain, and has yet to score for their senior side.)

But at the age of 18, and what earned the move to Spain, was how Jota scored a fairly incredible 12 league goals in just 31 games with unfashionable Paços de Ferreira (who sound more like a 1970s club singer than a football club). Not many teenagers get into double figures in the league aged 18 in modern football. By contrast, after a year in Sporting's first team and three full seasons at Manchester United, Cristiano Ronaldo, playing in a strong side, never once got into double figures in the league; Jota's goalscoring stats are far better by comparison. Of course, this merely shows how players can sometimes explode as goalscoring phenomena, and few will ever match the rate Ronaldo then started scoring at – but he also had a prolific youth record for Portugal U15s and U17s, if not with their U20s or U21s. As with Torres and Jota, there were clues in the international age-group figures.

Jota's two goals in a recent game for Portugal against Sweden (to make it three international goals already this season, at the start of his career at that level) – when replacing Covid-struck Ronaldo – cemented in my mind a comparison with Fernando Torres. There was something in the balance, and the striking of the ball.

Indeed, both finishes were in some way similar to his second goal against Atalanta – a real power and trueness in his strikes that Torres had, and which Mo Salah and Sadio Mané, great finishers as they are, don't quite consistently have. Jota's hat-trick goal, as he rounded the keeper, was also reminiscent of Torres, but the deftest little dink for the first wasn't too far from his style, either. There already feels like something pretty ruthless about Jota, even if he may just be starting on a high, like Salah in 2017/18, in contrast to the slow-burn players who took quite a few months to settle in (Roberto Firmino, Fabinho, Andy Robertson, Alex Oxlade-Chamberlain, et al). That said, even when he scored 44 goals, Salah was guilty of a lot of glaring misses; his game is more about quantity and quality of chances, rather than ruthlessness, bar the occasional super-hot finishing streak.

Jota's form meant that he started the game against Manchester City five days later. The game at The Etihad sparked into fast and furious life from the first whistle, with the Reds creating various promising openings in the opening few minutes, and, after taking the lead, continued to dominate for the first half an hour, before the game gradually petered out as the half wore on; and the second half descended into mostly two worn-out teams keeping possession, as the relentless schedule – made worse by the Champions League being condensed into a shorter period of time, along with all the other games – started to take a toll.

Neither manager was happy with the physical demands placed on the players. After the game, Jürgen Klopp said: "The Premier League has to change. Sky, BT, you – everyone has to talk to each other. You want good football? Give the boys a few hours more rest."

In the first half Liverpool were making incisive passes right into the heart of the City box, and in the second half the passes were in the same direction, as if the teams hadn't swapped ends at the interval – Alisson receiving countless back-passes as Liverpool, already lacking Virgil van Dijk, Fabinho, Thiago and several others from the first-team squad, lost Trent Alexander-Arnold to a calf injury after an hour; James Milner, now aged 87, facing up to Rahcem Sterling on the flank, in yet another patch-up job for Klopp (and Milner was canny enough to not get beaten once in a "foot race", although what other types of race you can have in a football match is hard to know; perhaps an "elbow race" to see who can stay onside longer?).

Klopp started with all four of the main attacking talents after the midweek hat-trick for Diogo Jota, and although Roberto Firmino still looked low on confidence and lacking in sharpness, he helped the Reds to flood forward against the hosts whilst also blocking the passing lanes of City's defence, which hemmed them in their own half. Liverpool took the lead with *another* penalty – reaching the 38-game average between 2018 and 2020 of four per season *in just eight games* – albeit Leicester City had already won a scarcely believable *eight* (incidentally, eight is also the most a Liverpool team managed by Klopp had won in an *entire season*), such was the proliferation of spot-kicks. Sadio Mané was too quick for Kyle Walker, and Walker, as he and his team-mates did against Leicester, fouled an attacker who had just cut past him into the box. Mo Salah made no mistake, to extend his 100% run to 14 spot-kicks, dating back to his second penalty in the Reds' colours, having missed his first.

But then City grabbed an equaliser out of nothing: Gabriel Jesus' first touch looking initially like a mis-control, but on replays it could be seen as a deliberate flick through his own legs, and that would explain why, even though three Liverpool players also reacted quickly, he was the only one who knew where the ball was going to land, and just beat them to it with a prod into the bottom corner. It was half an hour into the game, and the first attack of note from Pep Guardiola's men.

It wouldn't be the 2020/21 season for Liverpool without some farcical VAR calls, and suddenly a cross that struck Joe Gomez's arm as – whilst running (which requires, er, moving your arms) – he pulled his hand down to his side was given as handball; unthinkable until the recent rule changes, and still a travesty of the spirit of the laws, and the talk of the "natural silhouette" – which should surely be applied only to players making a deliberate attempt to make themselves bigger to block a shot or a cross. Gomez was trying to make his body *smaller*, not bigger, and by the time the ball struck him his arm was almost at his side.

Thankfully Kevin de Bruyne struck the penalty a yard wide, which spurred Liverpool on, as if they had themselves scored a goal. But with the interval imminent, there wasn't time to turn that resumed pressure into an advantage, and the second half was a total damp squib – with *damp*, in the fierce Manchester downpour, the operative word. (There was so much water on the pitch that a damp squid would not have looked out of place.)

It all meant that the Reds ended this section of the season, heading into the two-week international break, in 3rd place, a point off leaders Leicester and behind 2nd-placed Spurs on goal difference. By contrast, City were in 10th, Arsenal 11th and Manchester United 14th. Spurs' fixtures after the break would see them catch up on their Big Six clashes, with three in a row, before facing Liverpool at Anfield shortly after. As in previous seasons, the Reds had played the toughest games of anyone during the first quarter of the campaign, with three Big Six clashes in just eight games, plus the Merseyside derby. The ninth would be against early leaders Leicester, who were on course to treble the league record for number of penalties in a season.

Of the six traditionally toughest away games on paper, Liverpool had already gone to Stamford Bridge, Goodison Park and The Etihad, although in a trend across the league, away fixtures were proving less favourable to home sides with the lack of a partisan crowd. Even so, it was 50% of the toughest away games played in just the first 21% of the season. Liverpool had already played Arsenal as well, plus high-flyers Aston Villa, who beat the Gunners 3-0 at The Emirates in the last game before the interlude.

In addition to this, while the inclusion of Midtjylland gave Liverpool's Champions League group the look of an easier ride, Klopp's men had already gone to Ajax and Atalanta (the two toughest ties, against recent semi/quarter-finalists) in the first three match-weeks. It also meant more travelling had been undertaken, which would presumably be an increased factor in a season that felt like a quart squeezed into a pint pot, as the Reds' injuries piled up. By early November, across all competitions, Liverpool had already gone to Manchester City, Chelsea, Everton, Ajax and Atalanta, winning three (which should have been four after the Goodison VAR debacle) and drawing two, as well as beating Arsenal. Indeed, in the four aforementioned league games, the Reds were actually up on their points hauls from both the 97- and the 99-point seasons; and two away group wins in Europe was already an improvement on recent times, with one still to play.

The anomaly was the result at Villa Park, but their 3-0 win over Arsenal suggested maybe they are some kind of kryptonite to teams that play a certain way – with some additional luck thrown in. Add all the injuries to Klopp's squad, with some big names due to return when the season resumed after another stupidly packed international break, in addition to several ludicrous VAR decisions to make games harder (or cost points), and Liverpool were arguably as impressive as in the previous two campaigns – just presented with an even taller mountain to climb.

One thing Liverpool fans hadn't seen in 2020/21, and almost certainly *wouldn't* see, was the club's best XI on the pitch at the same time. The closest the club got in the opening portion of the season was Chelsea away, when Thiago came on at half-time to provide a record-breaking 45 minutes (in terms of touches of the ball for someone who played 45 minutes or less in a Premier League game), and Virgil van Dijk was fit and strong. With those two on the pitch the Reds won the second half (and the game) 2-0, albeit against ten men. Thiago then fell ill, but returned from a bout of Covid-19 to start the game that saw the Reds 1-0 up at Everton before van Dijk's season was ended by the reckless Pickford – after just ten minutes; albeit Adrián was in goal at the other end from the start, and not Alisson, so even that was Liverpool absent a key player. And that was also Thiago's last involvement for several weeks.

From that point on the side was always going to be understrength in some way or another, as van Dijk was the bedrock of the defence (and a potent attacking threat at set-pieces, as well as a deep-lying playmaker), but Klopp has never shied away from a 'make do and mend' attitude. With Fabinho, the 4th-choice centre-back, injured in the hectic schedule, Nat Phillips made his league debut for the Reds, aged 23, in the win against West Ham; and aerially at least, he compensated for the

Dutchman's absence, with a towering display. This was just days after it had been Rhys Williams, 19, replacing the Brazilian who was in turn replacing the Dutchman. Phillips wasn't even in the Champions League squad, as he was due to leave to join one of 12 interested Championship clubs, only for nothing to be sorted in time, as Swansea, the preferred destination, were only using Phillips as a backup if other deals fell through. Rhys Williams returned to the team against Atalanta, and in three group games the Reds had yet to concede a goal – albeit perhaps in part to taking the defensive line back after the Aston Villa drubbing, which made it harder to compress the midfield and stay joined-up as a team, but a balance had been struck, for the time being at least, in still being able to attack with enough numbers to win games. To get Thiago in the team would also allow for more of the accurate passes from deep that fell under van Dijk's purview.

In an echo of life from earlier in 2020, Liverpool came from behind against the Hammers as the Coronavirus situation worsened, and a national lockdown soon followed. This time football would not stop, although it would continue to be without fans.

But even the international break (which is still unfolding as I write) has been a nightmare. First, Joe Gomez's season was ended in England training when he dislocated his kneecap, and tore his patella tendon. So both of Liverpool's first-choice centre-backs saw their campaigns prematurely ended by ultra-serious knee injuries. Days later, Mo Salah tested positive for Covid-19 whilst in Egypt.

Virgil van Dijk finally underwent an operation, after the swelling had died down, and will be partnered by Gomez in their recuperation at the world-class replacement of Melwood – the new AXA Training Centre at Kirkby, built beside the Academy –

which the Reds belatedly moved into just before this book went to print.

It is yet another major step forward in the club's rise from sleeping giant to undoubted superclub in the past decade; from the lows of Roy Hodgson and terrible owners who had dropped the club into a relegation battle, to new custodians, Jürgen Klopp, and the claiming of the Champions League, Premier League and Club World Cup.

My Day At The Match: The View From Jail – Liverpool v Man City, 27th November 2011

Nabs Al Busaidi

Chairman, Oman Official Liverpool Supporters Club

In early November 2011, I was supposed to be on my way to the Antarctic, to walk to the South Pole. Days before the flight to South America, I was in London when I got a call saying my nephew had died. I was on a flight back to Oman three hours later, and the South Pole was put on hold, indefinitely.

When I got to my sister's house, my niece and I went into my nephew's room to clean it up as soon as we could. This was the analogue version of deleting his browser history. My sister, my nephew's mother, was also there, so we tried not to do this under her nose. The only relevant item to the story is that I found a few spent bullet cartridges, and palmed them, and then slid them into an outer pocket of my backpack.

(For those who do not know, generally a bullet consists of the metal projectile which comes out the barrel, and the brass cartridge, which is ejected sideways by the gun. The 'spent' cartridge is harmless, and is usually collected as a souvenir or scrap metal. It is not a danger to anyone unless you step on one in bare feet. But I palmed them anyway so that my sister didn't have more to worry about. She might have put two and two together and come up with armed insurrection. Understandably, she was not taking the loss of her first child very well.)

A couple of weeks later I flew to a nearby country for a few days. As with all my flights, I planned my flights around Liverpool's fixtures, so I was scheduled to fly back to Oman on 27th November 2011, with several hours spare, which was plenty of time to get home, change and get to the home of Oman Reds in the Grand Hyatt sports bar to watch the big clash between a revitalised team under Kenny Dalglish; against the newly financially doped-up Ivan Drago called Manchester City. City were unbeaten after 12 games, with 11 wins and a draw and were five points clear already. They had just humped Man United 6-1 the month before. This was definitely a game to look forward to.

A bit of context and some reminders: in October 2011, Suárez had clashed with Patrice Evra, but was not banned yet. King Kenny was the permanent manager, again. And this was the year City finally won the league with *Agguuuueeeerrrrroooooo*.

As I was going through the final x-ray before getting on the returning plane, the police discovered that I had three bullet cases in my backpack. I had totally forgotten I had stashed them in one of the outer pockets. Initially, I didn't think it was a big deal. Anyone with any knowledge of guns knows that the spent cartridges are as much use as jewellery, but that was not how the police were treating it. Airport security personnel have the most tedious job. Nothing of consequence ever happens at airport x-rays, except discovering a forgotten water bottle, and then being able to act really officious at discovering a potential water bomb. But this time, it was like they had finally, actually, really caught someone who might be in Al Qaeda. All those years of staring at an x-ray screen had finally paid off.

So, despite my explanations and saying they were more than welcome to confiscate them, I was arrested, hauled off to a minibus with several others, and taken to jail. I was still in my suit, and so the police did not bother to cuff me, whereas the others all looked like labourers and were hand-cuffed to each other. And crucially, I still had my Blackberry in my suit pocket. (It was 2011 so a Blackberry was pretty standard back then.)

I had no idea what was happening as I was told nothing, and I did not know what was going to happen to me, as no one would tell me anything, but I figured as soon as I was able to discuss my situation with someone in authority, they would see that this was a whole lot of nothing, and I could still catch my flight, and make it to the game, with just an interesting story to tell.

Looking back, it is interesting to note that my biggest concern at this point was missing the match....

At the holding jail, I was put into a room that was roughly two metres by three metres. Concrete walls on three sides and floor to ceiling iron bars on the fourth. Classic wild west jail cell. Except no window. And no bed. And no chairs. And there were 12 men already inside. Twelve miserable, downcast men. And I made it lucky 13. The floor was already taken with people sitting, so it was standing room only.

For some reason, I was still hopeful that my situation was a misunderstanding that just needed a quick explanation and I would be on my way. So, as I walked in, I was cheerful and greeted everyone and asked how they were doing. All 12 were manual labourers from the Indian sub-continent, and 11 of them didn't understand any English. But the 12th man did, so I struck up a conversation with him, and eventually asked him why he was in jail.

He had come from India to this country with the promise of a job, housing, pay etc. He had taken a loan to pay an agent to secure him the job, but once he arrived in the country, his passport was taken away, he was forced to share accommodation almost as cramped as our jail cell, and he was not paid for several months. He was desperate for food and money, so he ran away from his employer and started cleaning cars on the street to make ends meet with the hope of getting enough money to get out of the country. He was caught by the police and as he was reported as a runaway, he was arrested and was now awaiting deportation.

It was a terrible story. Totally unfair. I asked if he had reported his employer for breach of contract, but he laughed. It did not matter as the employer was a local national and therefore untouchable. But he was happy now. He would leave the country and never be allowed back. He still had massive debts back home with the agent, but it was better than staying.

I asked him about the man sitting next to him on the floor. They spoke in Hindi back and forth for several minutes, and his story was almost the same. Big promises. Big loan. Big lies. Cleaning cars to make ends meet. Caught and awaiting deportation. And his other neighbour. Same story. And every other person in the call. Same story. Different details, but the exact same substance. Each telling of their stories made me sadder, and angrier. Nothing changed except their name, and where they came from.

After that, we all stood or sat in silence, waiting for something to happen.

While waiting, I decided to surreptitiously message the British ambassador in Oman. We had known each other for a long time. He had been the UK ambassador in Bahrain before, and we became closer during the Arab Spring, when I volunteered as an emergency warden in case of the need to evacuate UK nationals. Now we were both based in Oman, so I thought I would let him know I was in prison, but didn't need assistance. Just someone to know where I was. And match updates, if required. Again, my biggest concern at this point was missing the match!

I had been standing for nearly two hours, and nothing seemed to be happening, so I hatched a little plan. I told the guards I needed to use the toilet. There was no toilet in the cell, and I could see no facilities for the prisoners, so I wanted to see how they would handle my request, and take it from there. One of the guards took me to the policeman's bathroom. He stood nearby while I stood at the urinal. I didn't actually need to go to the toilet, so while explaining that I had stage fright with him watching, it gave me the opportunity to talk to him, and hopefully make some type of connection.

He was from Syria, and all the non-commissioned policemen were from the poorer Arab countries – Egypt, Palestine, Jordan, Yemen etc. He had been in this country for seven years, and liked the place and his job. After a bit of bonding, I decided to test the waters. I asked him if he knew why the other men in my cell were arrested, and he did. But he said the real criminals were untouchable because they were locals, so they were only allowed to process the foreigners. It wasn't fair, but there was nothing he could do about it.

It was fair enough. He was low down on the totem pole, and just trying to get by in life. I managed to get a few more details out of him, and went back to the cell, where I found out my legal case had been referred urgently to the court for processing. Good news I thought. Still time to make the game.

I was taken to what looked like a converted school room and interrogated in Arabic by three men behind a long desk. The man who I guessed was my interpreter couldn't speak English, and I couldn't speak Arabic, so I didn't see this going well for me. In a fit of anger and frustration the middle of the three men broke into English and said I was being charged with terrorism, possession of illegal firearms and piracy.

Piracy of all things! They clarified that they meant air piracy – still, probably not the best time to laugh, but it was laughable.

And having laughed at them, it turned out the three men behind the desks were the judges, and the interpreter was my lawyer. My lawyer was trying to convince me to say I was guilty and beg for leniency! So, first things first, I told him he could *fuck right off*. I mean, I told him that I was very grateful for his time, but I would rather deal with this myself. Even if I couldn't speak Arabic, I couldn't represent myself any worse than this court-appointed lackey.

But in several coincidences of life-saving proportions, there was a lawyer present in the court whom I had met the day before. He came to my defence, not only with the ability to be able to speak English and Arabic, but also a newspaper article from that day's paper, with me in it, receiving an award from one of the most famous people in the country.

I explained the whole convoluted story of trying to find my nephew's porn stash after he died, and finding the used cartridges instead. But the part of the story that got them really agitated was that I claimed to have brought all three empty used cartridges all the way from Oman, through all the security checks on the outward journey, and then through half the security checks on the outward journey.

They suddenly realised that if my story was true, it would expose how ineffective the checks had been, in Oman and their own country. They questioned my story backwards and forwards, and couldn't find a flaw. The lawyer and I were getting more and more evidence to prove my innocence. So I was suddenly dismissed, as quickly as possible, and sent back to jail for out processing, which meant back to my two-by-three cell, but without my previous friends.

It was now several hours into my piracy drama, and there was no way I could get to Oman to watch the game. My best hope was to watch the game in this country. But out-processing seemed to move at a different pace than what I wanted and kick off arrived, and I was still incarcerated. I was stuck with using my contraband Blackberry to request updates from the Oman Reds watching the game.

I also tried to find out when I was being released, and whether I could watch the game. It was too much to hope that the police had a TV with match coverage, but one thing I have found in the 85 countries I have been to, men will like football, and they will probably watch the Premier League. Turns out my Syrian friend was a lot more helpful now that I was no longer under arrest, and although they didn't have a TV with coverage, they did have a computer which he would let me use … if I added him on Facebook!

Seemed like a fair trade. I still wasn't able to get a live feed, but I was able to get text coverage. For those of you who are old enough, this is the 21st century version of watching a match on Teletext.

Gary Speed had died that morning, apparently from suicide, and so the lively Craig Bellamy, his good friend, was not playing. But we had Suárez, and we had King Kenny managing. The match at Anfield started and it seemed to be all one way traffic. For City – after half an hour Vincent Kompany scored, and my heart sank when I saw that Joleon Lescott scored two mins later. A drubbing was on the cards ... except it was an own goal! The score was 1-1. The game was fairly quiet after that, at least according to Facebook updates and text commentary.

At half time, I asked my new police friends to slow down the paperwork, so that I could finish the second half before they released me. They were totally understanding, and asked for updates as well.

In the second half, the game seemed to be played on Red Bull. Chances were flying in so fast, I did not know who was getting the better of the match. Then Mario Balotelli came on. And then went off mins later, after two yellow cards. After that, it seemed to be one way traffic. I was doing my best to visualise a goal for Liverpool. Channelling my inner Secret, the texts were flying in fast.

Charlie Adam... Hart saves.

Kuyt... Hart.

Downing... Hart.

Suarez... Hart.

Carroll... Hart.

Suarez... Hart.

Downing... Hart.

And then it was the final whistle. Only the second team to take points off City in the league so far, but both teams left believing they should have had more.

The police out-processed me quickly after the game ended, but couldn't release me, as I had already gone through immigration, so I was taken back to the airport, and put into the transit area to wait for the next flight to Oman eight hours later…

Since 1998, I can probably count the number of Liverpool games I have missed for funerals, surgeries, expeditions … but this reason, arrested for piracy, is probably the most unusual, and one that I had conveniently forgotten until recently.

PS: Until I wrote this article, I had never seen the game, or even any highlights. After nine years, I felt I should, just to make sure my memory was not playing tricks on me, and Hart really did pull off some great saves to keep City in the game.

Unravelling the Rich and Varied DNA of Liverpool's Goals

By Andrew Beasley

Intro by Paul Tomkins

Halfway through last season I had the idea of creating a DNA database of Liverpool's goals – in response to the notion that the Reds only scored headers from set-pieces, which coincided with a run of four headed set-piece goals in late November/early December, but which then gave way to a dozen consecutive goals scored with fast and/or free-flowing football with barely a header anywhere in any of the moves.

These were at least two defining and yet deeply contrasting types of "Liverpool goal". Then there were other factors: the many goals scored from fast or clever throw-ins; the many goals that involved Virgil van Dijk at the start of a move; the many goals that involved the ball being switched fully from one flank to the other, and sometimes back again.

There were the slow moves; the fast moves; the short moves; the long moves. There were those that began with the goalkeeper, and those that came about from a final-third press. There were even goals – plural – that came from opposition corners. (Alas, there weren't many *penalties*. Have I mentioned how few penalties Liverpool get? At least the Reds have already gained four in 2020/21, albeit in a season of massively inflated penalty decisions.)

I didn't get the chance to finish the DNA project (which involved detailed video analysis from the start of each and every move, using scouting software), as Covid-19 struck and I spent time re-writing *Perched: Jürgen Klopp's Liverpool FC – Champions Of Everything*, before the season resumed, games came thick and fast, and there wasn't time to properly analyse the post-lockdown matches.

That said, I will be finishing the analysis in the coming weeks, and writing an article about the DNA of all of Liverpool's goals in 2019/20 (Premier League and Champions League).

However, I thought that it would be something that Andrew Beasley could take and run with for this season, and as such have asked him to do a monthly look at the various characteristics of the Reds' goals, and to build up a picture as the season unfolds. Andrew has found additional things to look at that hadn't occurred to me, and hopefully this will be a regular feature that paints a varied picture of the way that Liverpool get the goals that win lots of games.

Goals DNA: September and October 2020

While this concept is Paul's idea, I'll be writing about different things I happen to notice in the data each month. To begin, we'll be taking a look at the 20 goals which Liverpool scored in the league and in Europe in September and October. So sorry, Diogo, your hat trick in Italy will have to wait for the next roundup.

Penalties

After Liverpool only had six penalties in all competitions in the whole of last season, they've already had four in 2020/21. Hell, the two they had against Leeds on the opening weekend was double the total they had between December 27th and their final match of the last campaign.

And for the first time ever, Mohamed Salah has taken four in a row (or five including the final one of 2019/20), and has slotted them all home. The interesting thing is, all four of them have gone into a different sixth of the goal, as defined by Opta.

But it turns out this is nothing new. A tweet from Sam McGuire pointed out how Salah's penalty placement has been fairly varied across the 14 which he has taken for Liverpool (only the first of which was missed). I don't know why I'm always so nervous whenever Salah steps up for a penalty. He's near faultless from the spot and his placement is so varied. As per *Opta*'s classification, the Egyptian only has to score in the top left and top right to complete the set this season.

Set pieces

Despite being the top-scoring side from set plays over the last three seasons, the Reds only scored two in the first two months of 2020/21. And just as the penalties turned up like buses against

Leeds United, so did the goals from other dead-ball situations. Did two arms in the air mean 'aim for Virgil', Robbo?

Liverpool got nine assists directly from set plays in their title winning campaign – seven from corners and two from free-kicks – but only picked up one in our study. Virgil van Dijk's header against the Bielsa boys was one of four goals which the Reds scored from a maximum distance of five yards, though something differentiated it from the other three ....

Open goals

This section again calls upon the excellent *Statsbomb* data on FBRef.com. By their definition, Jürgen Klopp's team have scored three times when faced with an open goal this season, compared with only five in the league in the whole of the last campaign.

Each time the scorer was no more than five yards from goal which obviously makes sense, as a player is likely to have at least the goalkeeper blocking their route to glory most of the time. The only example from the 11 open goal shots the Reds took last season which was from further out occurred in the league derby at Anfield. Jordan Pickford raced to the edge of his area, Divock Origi knocked it past the idiot and found the back of the net from 11 yards to put Liverpool in front. Lovely stuff.

Perhaps the most interesting aspect of the three from 2020/21 is the game state at the time. The Reds were a goal down when they scored the first two examples, and level in the third. You would expect a team to perhaps score such goals when a game is stretched, with their opponents trying to get back into the contest, so to score while the other side has something definite to defend is worth a doff of the cap. Granted, two of the goals did feature rebounds following goalkeeper saves, but the player still needed to be in the right spot when it mattered.

Headers

The genesis of this project may have been to disprove the notion that Klopp's team only scored headers, but there's no doubt they have been important over the years. Liverpool scored 18 in the league last season – at least four more than every team, and over double the top flight average of around seven per club.

Having converted three in their opening seven games of this campaign, they may end 2020/21 with a similar total as last year. The absence of van Dijk will hinder that possibility of course, but aside from the Dutchman's strike against Leeds the other two were scored by Sadio Mané and Diogo Jota.

All three efforts eligible for this section were lead-taking goals too, showing that it's not just how many headers Liverpool score which has made such goals so important to their cause.

Throw-ins

When *The Tomkins Times* began, the notion of an article celebrating Liverpool goals from throw-ins would've been absurd. At that time it was the Pulisolithic era, when footballing dinosaurs instructed their team to launch every throw-in they won past the halfway line into the opposition's penalty area, to wreak havoc galore.

Thanks to Thomas Grønnemark, things have thankfully moved on. There are still idiots from the dark ages who mock, naturally, but Liverpool are happy to pick up a marginal gain wherever they can. As well as scoring from moves which began with throw-ins of their own, they even scored following one by the opposition. Perhaps Sheffield United should give Grønnemark a call if he ever decides to stop working with the Reds?

While none of the throw-ins made much direct impact into the goal scoring moves which followed (with the possible exception of the own goal in Amsterdam), it will be interesting to see how common such attacks are this season. And ultimately, Liverpool are now routinely retaining possession from throws when they rarely used to. Plus one of the quintet of goals the Reds scored in Bergamo *definitely* had a key involvement from a throw-in, but more on that next month.

Postage stamp

If you're a very long time TTT subscriber, you may recall '*Postage Stamp – How Important is Shot Placement*' almost nine years ago, which looked at how shots on target conversion rates vary by which part of the goal the ball is struck into. (I *essentially* invented post-shot expected goals, but I don't like to brag.) The findings helped to explain why Kenny Dalglish's side were struggling to score that season, even when they weren't doing their utmost to hit the woodwork. Wonderful times.

The research for the article, which covered several seasons of Premier League football, led to the creation of conversion rates by six zones within the goal.

The least successful section is the central zone of the bottom of the goal – it makes sense that this would be the case, but I'm pointing it out here as Liverpool's conversion rate in that zone has been 28% in the first two months of 2020/21, with seven goals scored from 25 shots, which is way above the long term average of 15.9%.

Unsustainable, or quality finishing? Ultimately we'll have to wait and see, but a closer look at the goals explains some of the success. One of the strikes was a penalty, and the other six were all from closer than 12 yards to goal. There were a couple of efforts into open goals, and another which took place when Mané made a mug of Kepa Arrizabalaga. Even so, I would expect the hit rate to drop as the season unfolds.

Passing sequences and involvement

While the average number of passes in the open play goal sequences has been just 5.1, there have been three which hit double figures, with 21 – in the build up to Andy Robertson's goal against Arsenal – the peak. When it comes to being involved in goal scoring moves (in any capacity, not just in terms of scoring or assisting) then this season there has been Salah, and then everyone else trailing in his wake.

Just six of the 20 goals saw no involvement from Salah, and even then there are explanatory circumstances for some of those in which he played no part; not least that he wasn't even on the pitch when Jota opened the scoring against FC Midtjylland, but it would also be tough to have any part in a corner headed home by van Dijk (without taking it of course), Mané's goal where he literally intercepted a pass from the opposing keeper, or an own goal which emerged shortly following a throw-in.

And while Salah has been the main man so far this season, he has an unfair advantage in being the first-choice penalty taker. Exclude the four spot kicks (now five in all competitions), and Trent Alexander-Arnold is only one involvement behind him, with Mané and Andy Robertson a further one back. It will be interesting to see what November brings.

Printed in Great Britain
by Amazon